Collins *Advanced Modular Science*

A2 OPTION

Applied Ecology

Manchester
Centre

Series Editor: Mike Bailey

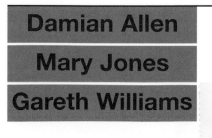

Damian Allen

Mary Jones

Gareth Williams

This book has been designed to support AQA Biology specification B.
It contains some material which has been added in order to clarify the
specification. The examination will be limited to material set out in the
specification document.

Published by HarperCollins*Publishers* Limited
77–85 Fulham Palace Road
Hammersmith
London
W6 8JB

www.CollinsEducation.com
Online support for schools and colleges

All new material in this book has been written by Mary Jones.
This book draws on some sections from *Food, Farming and Environment* by
Damian Allen and Gareth Williams.

British Library Cataloguing in Publication Data
A catalogue record for this publication is available from the British Library

Cover design by Chi Leung
Design by Jordan Publishing Design
Edited by Penelope Lyons
Illustrations by Barking Dog Art, Russell Birkett, Tom Cross and
Illustrated Arts
Picture research by Caroline Thompson
Index by Kathleen Lyle
Production by Kathryn Botterill
Commissioned by Martin Davies
Project edited by Simon Gerratt

Printed and bound in Great Britain by Scotprint

The publisher wishes to thank the Assessment and Qualifications Alliance
for permission to reproduce examination questions.

You might also like to visit
www.**fire**and**water**.com
The book lover's website

CONTENTS

Acknowledgements

Text and diagrams reproduced by kind permission of:
Wiltshire Trust for Nature Conservation; *Ecology*; Thomas Nelson & Sons Ltd.; *Science*;
Longman; Blackie Academic and Professional; *Phil. Trans. R. Soc. London B*; *Water Resources*;
Academic Press Inc.; Newnes Books; The Open University; AHS; Granada; British Agrochemical
Association; Royal Society for the Protection of Birds; ABAL; World Wildlife Fund; *Journal of
Zoology*; Butterworth & Co; MAFF; EU website; Longman Scientific and Technical; *Nature*;
Taylor & Francis; English Nature; Mauna Loa Observatory, Hawaii; The Stationery Office.

Every effort has been made to contact the holders of copyright material, but if any have been
inadvertently overlooked the publishers will be pleased to make the necessary arrangements at
the first opportunity.

The publishers would like to thank the following for
permission to reproduce photographs:
(T = Top, B = Bottom, C = Centre, L= Left, R = Right):

Associated Press, 27, 32;
John Bebbington FRPS (Field Studies Council), 10;
Bruce Coleman Ltd/J L G Grande, 62;
Richard Elston, 89;
English Nature/P Wakely, 93;
Environmental Images/R Brook, 22, P Ferraby, 23, P Addis,
  51R, P Rowlands, 72T, C Westwood, 77;
Holt Studios International/N Cattlin, 47, 50, 54, J Chalmers,
  51L;
Geoff Jones, 18, 37T, 88;
FLPA/Jurgen & C Sohns, 14, D P Wilson, 72C, P Reynolds, 75T;
Marwell Zoological Park, 87;

NHPA/Lutra, 25, A Rouse, 35L, A.N.T, 37C, A Bannister, 38R,
  N J Dennis, 38L, E A Janes, 75B, T Kitchen & V Hurst, 85,
  D Woodfall, 95;
www.osf.uk.com/A & S Carey, 16L, T Ulrich, 16C, H Hall, 34T,
  J A L Cooke, 38C, I West, 83;
RSPB Photo Library/M Hamblin, 42;
Royal Botanic Gardens, Kew, 86;
Science Photo Library, 91, 98;
Still Pictures/D Watts, 34C, R Seitre, 35R, D Garcia, 82, David
  Woodfall, 6, 46, 78;
Woodfall Wild Images/C Preston, 17, S Scott, 68.

Front cover:
Images supplied by: Holt Studios International/N Cattlin (top
  left),
GettyOne Stone (centre), Science Photo Library (top right)

To the student

This book aims to make your study of advanced science successful and interesting. Science is constantly evolving and, wherever possible, modern issues and problems have been used to make your study stimulating and to encourage you to continue studying science after you complete your current course.

Using the book

Don't try to achieve too much in one reading session. Science is complex and some demanding ideas need to be supported with a lot of facts. Trying to take in too much at one time can make you lose sight of the most important ideas – all you see is a mass of information.

Each chapter starts by showing how the science you will learn is applied somewhere in the world. At other points in the chapter you may find more examples of the way the science you are covering is used. These detailed contexts are not needed for your examination but should help to strengthen your understanding of the subject.

The numbered questions in the main text allow you to check that you have understood what is being explained. These are all short and straightforward in style – there are no trick questions. Don't be tempted to pass over these questions, they will give you new insights into the work. Answers are given in the back of the book.

This book covers the content needed for the option module in AQA Specification B in Biology at A2-level: Module 6 – Applied Ecology. The Key Facts for each section summarise the information you will need in your examination. However, the examination will test your ability to apply these facts rather than simply to remember them. The main text in the book explains these facts. The case studies encourage you to apply them in new situations.

Words written in bold type appear in the glossary at the end of the book. If you don't know the meaning of one of these words check it out immediately – don't persevere, hoping all will become clear.

Past paper questions are included at the end of each chapter. These will help you to test yourself against the sorts of questions that will come up in your examination.

1 Diversity

When an ecologist begins to study an ecosystem, there are almost always three questions that need to be answered. These are:

- What organisms live there?
- Where do these organisms live?
- How many of them are there?

In order to answer these questions, numerical data must be collected from the ecosystem. The data which you collect, and the way in which you collect them, will be determined by the precise questions that you want to answer.

In this chapter, we will look at several different methods of collecting data, and some of the ways in which these data can be used to give us answers to particular questions about the ecosystem. We will also consider some of ways in which living organisms in an ecosystem interact with each other and with their environment, and how this may affect their diversity, distribution and abundance. You will need to know these ecological terms:

- **population** all the organisms belonging to one species that live in the same place at the same time and – if they reproduce sexually – that can interbreed with one another;
- **community** all the organisms of all species that live in the same place at the same time;
- **habitat** a place where organisms live;
- **niche** the role or way of life of an organism in an ecosystem – the ways in which it interacts with its physical environment and with other organisms;
- **ecosystem** all the living organisms and all the non-living components in a particular area that interact with each other and form a recognisable self-contained entity.

This sign is part of a woodland education scheme at Roeburndale Woods in Lancashire. Before such a scheme can be set up, information about the ecology of the site has to be collected and analysed.

1.1 Sampling techniques

You will probably already have studied an ecosystem yourself, and will have attempted to answer some or all of the questions above. If you had an infinite amount of time, and an infinite number of willing assistants to help you to collect the data, it might just be possible – in a very small ecosystem – to count and record every individual that lived there. In reality, however, this is simply not possible. Instead, we use various **sampling techniques**, attempting to do so in such a way that the results we obtain are genuinely representative of the habitat.

Random and systematic sampling

There are many ways of collecting information about the organisms living in a particular habitat, some of which are described below. But whatever sampling technique you decide on, you will need to decide whether to use random sampling or systematic sampling.

Random sampling means that you do not make any conscious decision about where the samples are taken. Random sampling ensures that each part of, say, a meadow has an equal chance of being sampled. This is often the best thing to do where the distribution of species within the area you are interested in is fairly uniform. For example, you may want to know what species of plants are present in a meadow and the relative areas of ground covered by each one. If it looks as though the meadow has fairly similar vegetation growing all over it, then a random sample should give you data that are representative of the whole meadow. This would also be the best thing to do if there were obvious patches of different vegetation – perhaps clumps of nettles – that were distributed randomly throughout the meadow.

One method of obtaining a random sample is to use a set of random numbers, either taken from a book or generated by a computer, to tell you where to put the

quadrat. The numbers are used as coordinates on a pair of imaginary graph axes along two edges of your sampling area, as shown in Fig. 1a. You place your quadrat at the intersection of these coordinates.

Systematic sampling means that you decide where to take your samples, and take them at regular intervals within the area you are interested in. You might decide, for example, to take a map of the meadow and to draw a set of grid lines on it, intersecting each other at right angles at regular intervals (Fig. 1b). You then count and record what is growing at each of these intersections. This could be useful if you were planning to come back and sample the same area again to find out if any changes had taken place, as you can be sure that your second sample is taken in the same places as the first one.

Another reason for deciding on systematic rather than random sampling is that you can see a gradation of some kind in the habitat, and you want to know more about it. For example, it may be apparent that the species growing in the meadow gradually change as you move from a dry part into a wetter part, or from the meadow into the edge of adjoining woodland. In these instances, you might choose to sample along a line that runs through these changing areas, allowing you to collect data about any changes in the species present, and their numbers, as the habitat changes. Such a line is called a **transect**, and is described more fully on page 9.

Frame quadrats

A **quadrat** is a defined area within which you collect data. The quadrat is placed on the ground, and you then identify and record the organisms inside it. Quadrats are the usual way of collecting data about which plants are growing in a habitat. They can also be used for **sessile** animals – that is, animals that are immobile for long periods of time, such as limpets and sea anemones. You have probably used some type of **frame quadrat**, a square frame that you place on the ground, then identify and count the organisms inside it (Fig. 2 overleaf).

Exactly what you record in your quadrats, and how you record it, depends both on the kind of organisms that are there, and what you intend to do with the data. The most obvious data to record are the numbers of individuals of each species inside the quadrat.

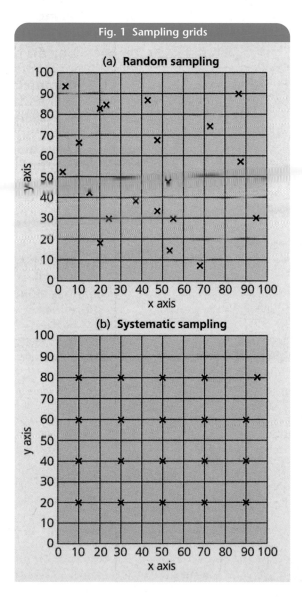

Fig. 1 Sampling grids

(a) Random sampling

(b) Systematic sampling

Fig. 2 Frame quadrats

Quadrats can be made from wood, wire or plastic.

Larger quadrats, for example for sampling in woodland, can be laid out with string and pegs.

All the species within a quadrat can be counted, or the abundance of each species estimated.

50 cm

50 cm

A quadrat with sides of 0.5 m has an area of 0.25 m². Wire fixed at 10 cm intervals gives 25 smaller units, each of 0.01 m², to make counting easier.

This could be appropriate, for example, if you wanted to know what animals were living on a seashore and the sizes of their populations.

It can sometimes be possible to record data about plants in this way, for example on an area of disturbed soil in a garden that had weeds growing on it. However, in many cases it is simply not possible to tell where one individual plant ends and another starts. In this instance, it is better to estimate the percentage of the area inside the quadrat that is occupied by each species. This is known as **percentage cover**. To help you to judge this, it is useful to divide a quadrat into several smaller ones (Fig. 3).

A third method is to use some kind of **abundance scale**. The ACFOR scale is a frequently used example in which you record each species as being abundant, common, frequent, occasional or rare. You can make an abundance scale semi-quantitative by relating it to percentage cover, for example by making A equal to 80–100% cover, C equal to 60–80% cover and so on down the scale.

1 Suggest the advantages and disadvantages of using the ACFOR scale, rather than estimating percentage cover.

Point quadrats
Estimating percentage cover, even in a quadrat divided into many smaller ones, is not easy to do accurately; and the larger the quadrat, the more difficult it gets. One solution is to make the quadrat so small that

its area is a single point. Such a quadrat is known as a **point quadrat**. Fig. 4 shows a frame that can be used for sampling with point quadrats.

Point quadrats are an excellent way of determining the percentage cover of all the different plant species in an area of relatively short vegetation. You can use random numbers to determine where to place the point quadrat frame. Then you drop the first needle through its hole, and count what it touches on its way to the ground – that is, the species that are present in the tiny quadrat represented by the end of the needle. If the vegetation is quite thick, with a mix of tall and short plants, the point may touch more than one species. You repeat this with all the other needles in the frame, and then repeat the whole exercise over and over again in the habitat. You can then work out the percentage of times you scored a 'hit' for any particular species, and this gives you the percentage cover of that species in that habitat. As leaves can lie above one another and you can hit more than one plant with each point, the percentage cover will probably add up to more than 100%.

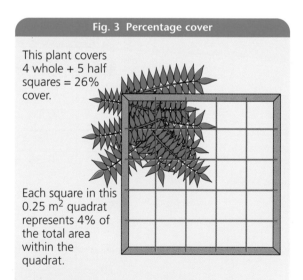

Fig. 3 Percentage cover

This plant covers 4 whole + 5 half squares = 26% cover.

Each square in this 0.25 m² quadrat represents 4% of the total area within the quadrat.

To measure percentage cover:

- lay a frame quadrat over the selected area;

- count the number of whole and half squares occupied by the species;

- calculate this as a percentage of the whole area of the quadrat;

- repeat for all the other species in the quadrat.

Point quadrats can be a much more objective and repeatable way of collecting data from which to calculate percentage cover, than frame quadrats, especially in relatively short vegetation. However, they are not so useful where the vegetation is long and

thick, because the needle may touch so many leaves on its way to the ground that you have difficulty in determining what it did hit and what it did not.

Line and belt transects

If you have decided to use a transect to collect data, then you need to consider whether it is better to use a **line transect** or a **belt transect** (Fig. 5). In either case, you begin by running a tape or piece of string along the line you are going to sample. If you are using a line transect, you then count and record individual organisms that are touching the tape. If the vegetation is very sparse, you could record every single individual. More usually, however, this is impractical, and you will need to choose a suitable interval along the tape – say, every 10 cm – at which to do this.

For a belt transect, you place frame quadrats so that one edge lies against the tape, and record the organisms within each quadrat. Once again, in some cases you might decide to record all along the tape, not missing out anything. Alternatively, if this would be too time-consuming, you can place the quadrats at equal intervals along the tape, perhaps every two metres. This is known as an **interrupted belt transect**.

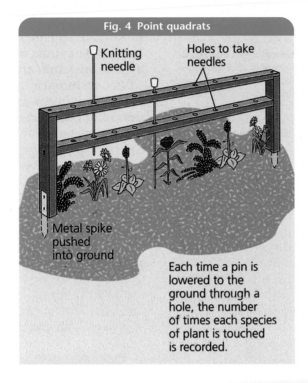

Fig. 4 Point quadrats

Knitting needle

Holes to take needles

Metal spike pushed into ground

Each time a pin is lowered to the ground through a hole, the number of times each species of plant is touched is recorded.

Fig. 5 Line and belt transects

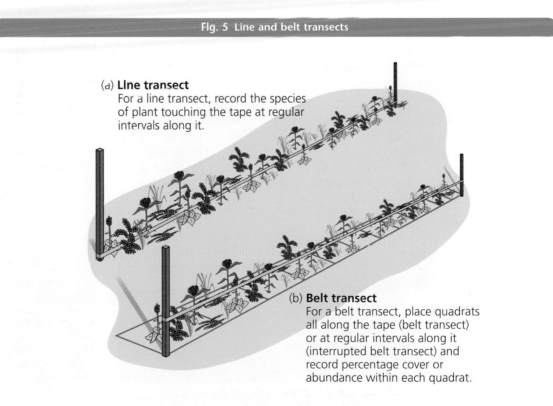

(a) **Line transect**
For a line transect, record the species of plant touching the tape at regular intervals along it.

(b) **Belt transect**
For a belt transect, place quadrats all along the tape (belt transect) or at regular intervals along it (interrupted belt transect) and record percentage cover or abundance within each quadrat.

Netting

Quadrats are a very good way of sampling anything that stays in one place. They can be used for collecting data about plants and sessile animals. Many seashore animals are sessile, and quadrats are an excellent way of investigating the distribution and abundance of seaweeds and animals on a rocky shore. However, the shore is a relatively unusual situation, and in most cases you will need to find different methods for collecting data about animals. In a meadow, for example, you would be most unlikely to find a short-tailed field vole sitting in the middle of your quadrat, even though these animals might be very common.

In grassland, you can collect samples of insects and other invertebrates using **sweep netting**. A standard technique should be used, always using the same size of net and moving it through the vegetation in the same way.

Nets are also useful for sampling aquatic organisms. In a stream or river, you can use a technique called **kick sampling**. You hold the net with its mouth facing into the water flow, as you stand upstream of it and disturb the mud or stones on the bottom with one foot. Again, you should use a standard technique, moving your foot in the same way and for the same length of time, in each area that you sample. In still water, you could use a technique similar to sweep netting, pulling your net through the water in a systematic way.

Trapping

Nets do not catch everything that lives in a habitat. Even sweep netting is unlikely to catch a vole in a meadow. In terrestrial habitats, some kind of trap is often used to collect larger and more mobile animals. Four different kinds of trap are shown in Fig. 6.

Longworth traps are used to catch small mammals such as mice and voles. The animal is not harmed by the trap, but it is very important to check traps at least once a day, so that any trapped animals can be released quickly. Individual animals that have been trapped are usually marked in some way, often by clipping away a small area of hair. In this way, you can tell whether or not a particular animal has been caught before.

Sweep netting works best in relatively long vegetation, and can be used successfully amongst shrubs and the lower branches of trees.

Kick sampling dislodges animals that are carried into the net by the water current.

A **pitfall trap** is simply a container that is sunk into the soil, into which invertebrates fall as they move over the ground. Slow-moving invertebrates can be caught in a **cover trap**, and some flying insects can be trapped in a **water trap**. Night-flying moths are attracted to a bright light such as a mercury vapour lamp, which can be arranged so that the moths fall into a container from which they can be retrieved the next morning.

Data from traps are not usually reliable enough to determine accurately how many different species of animals live in a habitat, nor to make anything better than a rough estimate of the sizes of their populations. For example, some mammals may be much more wary of Longworth traps than others. Some individuals become 'trap-happy', returning night after night to find the food that they have learnt is inside a trap. Another potential

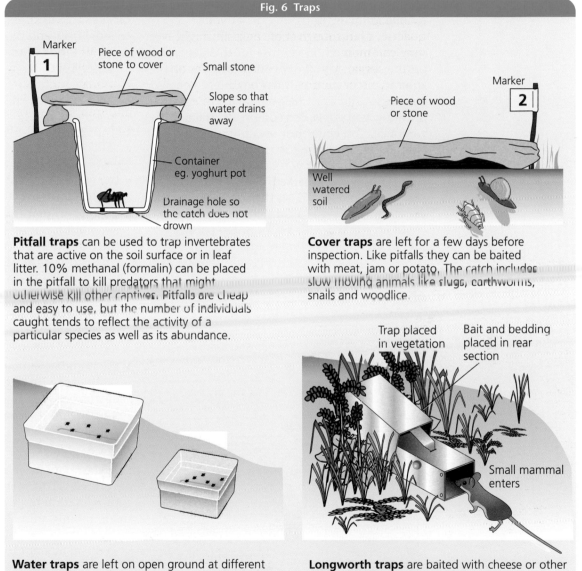

Fig. 6 Traps

Pitfall traps can be used to trap invertebrates that are active on the soil surface or in leaf litter. 10% methanal (formalin) can be placed in the pitfall to kill predators that might otherwise kill other captives. Pitfalls are cheap and easy to use, but the number of individuals caught tends to reflect the activity of a particular species as well as its abundance.

Cover traps are left for a few days before inspection. Like pitfalls they can be baited with meat, jam or potato. The catch includes slow moving animals like slugs, earthworms, snails and woodlice.

Water traps are left on open ground at different heights. Yellow traps seem to attract aphids while white attracts flies. They can be made from old ice cream cartons, half filled with water. Some washing up liquid can be added to reduce the surface tension so that insects landing on the water will sink.

Longworth traps are baited with cheese or other food, and left in long grass where small mammals are likely to be found. As the animal enters, it triggers a lever which allows the trap door to close behind it. The trap should contain warm, dry bedding so that the animal comes to no harm before the trap is revisited and the animal released.

Source: Adapted from Wiltshire Trust for Nature Conservation

problem is that, if you set a pitfall trap in the evening and collect its contents next morning, you may find one rather fat predatory beetle, and nothing else. Short of doing an analysis of the beetle's stomach contents, you will never know what else had fallen into the trap. However, you can put alcohol into the bottom of the trap, so that everything that falls in is killed straight away.

The mark–release–recapture technique

The **mark–release–recapture** technique is used for estimating the size of a population of mobile animals (Fig. 7).

First, a large number of the animals are caught. The method you use for this depends on the species you are investigating. For an aquatic insect such as water boatmen, you could use nets. For small mammals in a meadow, you could use Longworth traps. For woodlice, you could just search under stones and pieces of decaying wood.

The animals that you have caught are counted and then marked. The method of marking also depends on the species you are working with. Water boatmen or woodlice could be marked with a spot of red paint, small mammals by clipping their fur.

Whatever you choose, try to ensure that it will not increase the likelihood of the marked animals being eaten by predators.

The marked animals are then released back into their original habitat. Give them enough time to mix thoroughly with the rest of the population, then catch another large sample using the same method. Count the total number of marked and unmarked animals in the second sample.

You can now calculate the size of the population using a formula called the **Lincoln Index**:

$$\text{total number of animals in population} = \frac{\text{number in sample 1} \times \text{number in sample 2}}{\text{number of marked animals in sample 2}}$$

An easy way of remembering this is that you multiply the two biggest numbers together, and divide by the smallest one.

This method only gives you relatively reliable results if:

- the original number of animals caught and marked is large;
- there is no significant immigration into, or emigration out of, the population between the collection of the first sample and the collection of the second sample;
- the marked animals are no more or less likely to die than the unmarked ones;
- the marked animals do mix fully and randomly into the population after they have been released;
- the population does not change significantly in size as a result of births or deaths between the capture of the first sample and the capture of the second sample.

It is probably almost impossible to be certain that your data meet all of these criteria, but nevertheless this method can give a useful approximation of population sizes for many small, mobile animals.

Fig. 7 The mark–release–recapture technique

Catch a large sample of the animals you want to study and count them.

Mark each animal in a way that will not harm it or attract predators.

Release the marked animals back into their habitat, and allow one or two days for them to mix with the rest of the population.

Catch a second large sample, and count the total number caught, along with the number of these that have already been marked from the first sample.

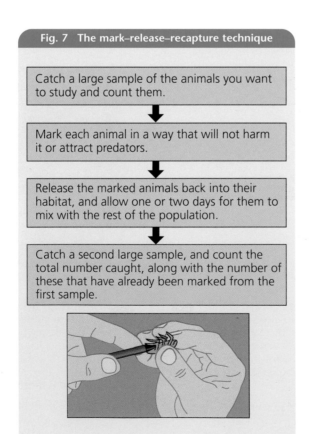

2 In an attempt to measure the size of a population of woodlice under a large piece of dead wood, a student captured and marked 54 animals. She released them and waited 48 hours before capturing another sample of 63 animals. Of these, 18 were marked. Use the Lincoln Index to estimate the number of woodlice in the population.

1.2 Diversity index

Ecologists studying an ecosystem often want to know the range of different species that live there. The more species there are, the stronger the argument for conserving the habitat.

A very simple statistic is the number of different species that live in a particular habitat. This is called the **species richness**. However, this does not tell you anything about the relative sizes of the populations of each species. A measure of **species diversity** takes into account not only how many different species there are in a habitat, but also the relative sizes of the populations, and how well the species are spread through the habitat. A meadow with 20 plant species, in which nearly all the plants belong to 6 species and the other 14 are very rare, or all clumped in one corner, will have the same species *richness* as another meadow in which all 20 species are fairly common and are found all over the meadow. But the first meadow has a smaller species *diversity* than the second.

Although it is easy to get a general idea of what species diversity means, there are no universally accepted definitions of it. There are many formulae for calculating species diversity. One commonly used example is **Simpson's Diversity Index**. The formula for calculating this is:

$$D = \frac{N(N-1)}{\Sigma n(n-1)}$$

where
D = Simpson's Diversity Index

N = the total number of individuals recorded in the sample
Σ = the sum of
n = the number of individuals of each species.

The larger the value for Simpson's Diversity Index, the greater the species diversity in the habitat.

If you are going to calculate this index, then you need to collect your data in a suitable way. As the formula includes the *number* of individuals counted, then you would imagine that you need to count *numbers*, rather than using percentage cover. However, as we have discussed, this is often impossible with plants. You can 'cheat' a little, by using point quadrats to collect your data, and counting each 'hit' as representing an individual plant. You will need to use a large number of point quadrats if your data are to be at all reliable.

Table 1 shows data taken from sampling a regularly mowed but rather weedy lawn. The values for n are the number of hits on that species.

$$\text{So, } D = \frac{232 \times 231}{10528}$$
$$= 5.09$$

Table 1 Data from 200 randomly placed point quadrats on lawn			
Species	**n**	**n–1**	**n(n–1)**
Grass species 1	80	79	6320
Grass species 2	45	44	1980
Clover	9	8	72
Black medick	22	21	462
Daisy	13	12	156
Dandelion	3	2	6
Germander speedwell	10	9	90
Self-heal	14	13	182
Moss	36	35	1260
Total (N) = 232		Total n(n–1) = 10528	

3 Using the method described above, a student collected the following data from a grass field grazed by sheep.

Grass	185
Thistles	28
Stinging nettles	35
Moss	2

a Arrange these data in a table that will allow you to calculate Simpson's Diversity Index.

b Calculate the index, showing your working.

c Explain why, when 200 point quadrat samples were taken, the value of N is more than 200.

d How does the species diversity of the field compare with that of the lawn? Suggest reasons for the differences between them.

e How reliable do you consider that this comparison is?

- Sampling in an ecosystem can be random, for example placing quadrats using random numbers. Alternatively, sampling may be systematic, using grids or transects.

- Frame quadrats can be used to define the area of ground sampled. Data can be collected about what species are present, their numbers or their percentage cover.

- Point quadrats are like frame quadrats with a very tiny area. Point quadrats are more objective than frame quadrats, as you do not have to make judgements about percentage cover of different species.

- Transects are used to investigate changes in species composition and abundance along a line where habitat and communities change.

- The choice of methods for collecting data depends partly on the habitat and species present, and also on the purpose for which you want to use the data.

- For motile animals where quadrats or transects cannot provide data, nets or traps can be used for sampling. If trapped animals are marked, released and recaptured, population size can be calculated using the Lincoln Index.

- Species diversity can be calculated using Simpson's Diversity Index.

1.3 Abiotic and biotic factors affect distribution and abundance

What determines which species live in a particular habitat, and the sizes of their populations? It may be simply be that a species has never arrived at that habitat. For example, although all polar bears live in the Arctic, and all penguins south of the equator, it is likely that polar bears could thrive in the Antarctic, and penguins could live successfully in high northern latitudes. The reason that they do not is that they have never dispersed into those regions.

Often, the reasons for the absence of a species from a particular habitat are that certain features of that habitat make it unsuitable for the species to live there. Features such as availability of food and range of temperatures are known as **ecological factors**, and they have a great influence on the distribution and abundance of organisms. Within any ecosystem, a very large number of ecological factors can be identified. It is helpful to classify these into abiotic and biotic factors.

Abiotic factors

Abiotic factors result from non-living parts of the ecosystem. They include temperature, light intensity, availability and salinity of water, and availability of gases such as carbon dioxide and oxygen. Most features of the soil, known as **edaphic factors**, are abiotic factors, and include the mineral content of the soil, its pH, and its water-holding and drainage capacities.

Giraffes do not live in the Arctic because they would not be able to find food there, and because they could not survive such cold temperatures.

Within any particular habitat, abiotic factors can vary hugely from place to place. In a hedgerow for example, light intensity is relatively high at the top of the hedge, much lower at the base, and practically zero beneath a stone lying among the hedgerow shrubs. Variations in temperature are highest at the top of the hedge, and much lower under the stone. Humidity, too, will vary most at the top of the hedge, but remain much more constant – and often be higher – beneath the stone.

The different areas within a habitat each have their own **microclimate**. Variations in microclimates within a habitat have great influences on distribution of different species within the habitat. For example, invertebrates such as woodlice, which are not very efficient at reducing water loss from their bodies, would not survive for long if they perched on a leaf at the top of the hedge, in full sunlight and fully exposed to drying winds. The microclimate beneath the stone, however, is ideal for them, and this is where you are most likely to find them.

Biotic factors

Biotic factors result from living components of the ecosystem. They include availability of food, competition, predation, parasitism and disease.

Living organisms require a range of resources in order to survive. If any one of these resources is in short supply, then organisms requiring that resource have to compete with each other in order to obtain it. Competition is frequently a major factor that affects the distribution and the population size of organisms.

Imagine a grassy meadow. The plants in the meadow all need light. The taller a plant is, the more light it is able to obtain. Shorter plants are shaded by taller ones, and receive less light. If the soil is rich in nutrients, then the taller plants such as some of the more vigorous grasses, thistles and docks will grow so large and shade the smaller plants so much that these are unable to thrive. Small, less vigorous plants such as orchids or cowslips may disappear completely from the meadow. The result of this competition has been to affect the distribution of the smaller plants. In this example, the resource in short supply is light. The plants competing for it belong to different species, so this is an example of **interspecific competition**.

Competition also occurs between individuals of the same species, and is then known as **intraspecific competition**. Fig. 8 shows the results of sowing different numbers of seeds into small pots of soil. You can see that the more seeds are sown in the pot and,

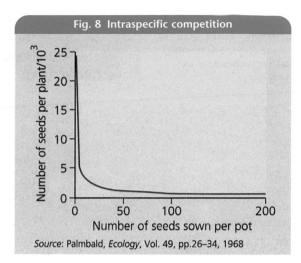

Fig. 8 Intraspecific competition

Source: Palmbald, *Ecology*, Vol. 49, pp.26–34, 1968

therefore, the larger the numbers of plants that grow in it, the fewer seeds these plants manage to produce. The plants are probably competing with each other for water and mineral ions from the soil, and also for light. The effect of this competition has been to reduce the reproductive capacity of each individual plant.

Intraspecific competition occurs whenever a population rises to a level that is near to the maximum that can be sustainably supported in a particular habitat. This maximum level is known as the **carrying capacity** for that species in that habitat. Interspecific competition occurs whenever two different species living in the same habitat require the same resource, and when this resource is in short supply. The more similar the niches of the two species, the more likely it is that interspecific competition will occur between them. If niches of two species are identical or extremely similar, then it is probably impossible for the two species to coexist. This is known as the 'competitive exclusion principle'.

The severity of **predation** on a population is, like interspecific competition, an example of a biotic factor acting between species. For example, hedgehogs are predators of slugs. If there are large numbers of hedgehogs in a garden, this could help to keep the population size of the slugs smaller than it would otherwise be. On the other hand, the size of a predator population may be influenced by the size of the prey population. Records for the number of skins of Canadian lynx (predator) and snowshoe hare (prey) sold to the Hudson Bay Company go back to 1845. They show regular fluctuations with changes in the lynx population lagging behind changes in the hare population (Fig. 9).

Parasitism and **disease** are very similar to predation in the ways in which they affect population sizes. Imagine a rabbit population living on a grassy hillside, where the rabbits spend much of their time resting and hiding from predators inside burrows. As their population increases, the rabbits become more and more crowded in their burrows. It gets much easier for disease-causing organisms such as the virus that causes myxomatosis, or for parasites, to spread from one animal to another. Moreover, the individual rabbits may be less able to fight off disease or parasites, because competition for food means that some of them may be undernourished. Therefore, as the rabbit population size increases, so the incidence and severity of disease and infection with parasites increases too. The rabbit population falls. When it reaches a lower level, disease and parasitism become less common and less severe, allowing the population to rise again.

Density-dependent and density-independent factors

Both abiotic and biotic factors can have a major influence on the population size of a particular species in a particular ecosystem. However, the kind of influence that each has is different.

Abiotic factors tend to have similar effects on a population whatever its size. They are described as **density-independent factors**, meaning that they are not affected by the size, or density, of a population. For example, if there is a very cold winter, then many small birds such as wrens may be killed. The effect is the same whatever the population size of the wrens to begin with.

Biotic factors, on the other hand, tend to have a greater effect on large populations than on small ones. They are described as **density-dependent factors**. For example, we have seen that, if a population of rabbits rises very high, then the spread and severity of disease increases. At the same time, the intensity of intraspecific competition for any resource that is in short supply, such as food, becomes more intense. The increasing shortage of food, and the increasing incidence of disease or infection with parasites, are likely to increase the death rate of the rabbits, and also reduce their reproductive rate. So the population size falls, thus reducing the intensity of intraspecific competition.

Of course, things are rarely so simple. Usually, a number of different factors, both abiotic and biotic, will interact and affect population sizes. For example, in a very cold winter (an abiotic factor) rabbits need more food to maintain their body temperatures, so that competition for food (a biotic factor) will become more intense. Indirectly, therefore, the abiotic factor is having a density-dependent effect on the rabbit population. In most cases that have been studied in natural ecosystems, it has proved almost impossible to identify which of many different biotic and abiotic factors are having the greatest influence on a population. An example is described in the following case study.

| Fig. 9 Population fluctuations in Canadian lynx and snowshoe hare |

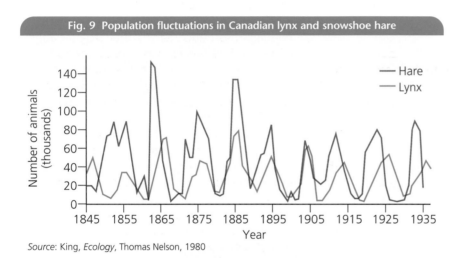

Source: King, *Ecology*, Thomas Nelson, 1980

A Canadian lynx stalking prey.

A Canadian snowshoe hare.

Red grouse populations

Red grouse, *Lagopus lagopus scoticus*, live on heather moorlands. They spend much of their time on the ground, where they feed on heather.

The population size of red grouse tends to swing up and down, oscillating widely over a period of about four or five years. Several theories have been put forward to try to explain what is causing the fluctuations. Whatever it is must be a density-dependent factor. As the grouse population increases, this factor increases too, and causes the population to decrease. As the population decreases, the factor decreases, allowing the population to increase again.

Suggestions for this density-dependent factor have included food supply and predation. However, neither of these seem to be the answer. Grouse eat around 2–3% of the available heather, so supply of heather is very unlikely to be affecting them. And predators, such as foxes and birds of prey, do not seem to take enough grouse to have such large effects. Two more likely possibilities are intraspecific competition for

space, and interactions between the red grouse and a parasite.

Competition for space arises during the autumn, when each breeding male takes control of an area of moorland. Territorial behaviour in autumn determines the number of breeding birds the following spring: the more aggressive the male grouse, the bigger their territories, the greater the emigration rate and the lower the number of breeding pairs. It is possible that aggression of the males is related to population density – the bigger the population, the more aggressive the males become, thus reducing the population size next year.

The second theory is to do with a parasite of red grouse, a nematode worm called *Trichostrongylus tenuis*. This parasite reduces growth of grouse populations by decreasing breeding rates. Both the rate and intensity of infection by the parasite increase as the population density of the birds increases. Evidence for this comes from studies showing:

- both grouse and *T. tenuis* have similar cyclical population densities;
- higher levels of parasite infection match greater losses from the grouse population;
- some grouse populations do not have any parasites, and their numbers do not oscillate.

During the 1980s and 1990s, six different grouse populations, living on six different areas of moorland in northern England, were investigated. First, using long-term data about grouse populations, predictions were made about when the next population 'crashes' would occur: 1989 and 1993. In 1989, the grouse in four of the six populations were caught and treated with a worm-killing drug. Two of the treated populations were then treated again in 1993. The graph on the left shows the results for three of the six populations.

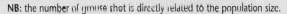
NB: the number of grouse shot is directly related to the population size.

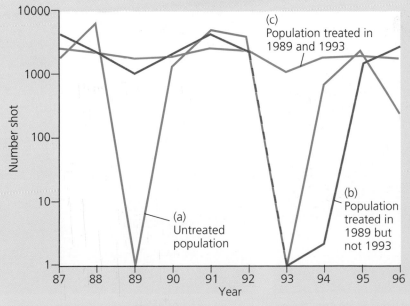

(c) Population treated in 1989 and 1993

(a) Untreated population

(b) Population treated in 1989 but not 1993

Source: Hudson et al., *Science* **282**, 1998

1 a Explain how these results support the hypothesis that the parasite is responsible for the cyclical fluctuations in red grouse populations.

b What evidence is there from these results that the nematode parasite may not be the only cause of these fluctuations?

1.4 Stability of ecosystems

Whenever ecologists attempt to find detailed explanations of the factors that are affecting and controlling population size of a particular species, they find a different picture. The interactions between populations and the different ecological factors that affect them are complex, and it is very difficult to make generalisations about them. However, one generalisation that does usually seem to hold true is that the relative importance of abiotic and biotic factors is different in harsh environments compared with less hostile ones.

Diversity and environment

A hostile environment is one in which it is not easy for organisms to survive; an example is a hot desert. In such conditions, only plants and animals that have evolved adaptations to enable them to cope with the lack of water and large temperature range can survive. (We will look at some of these adaptations in Chapter 3.) There are relatively few such organisms, and their population sizes tend to be fairly small. Diversity is low. In a hostile environment, the distribution and abundance of the organisms are largely determined by their ability to deal with the abiotic factors in the habitat. Biotic factors are relatively unimportant.

At the other end of the scale are habitats such as tropical rainforests that provide ideal conditions for plant and animal life. In such a habitat, huge numbers of species are able to survive. Diversity is very high. In this kind of place, abiotic factors are relatively unimportant in determining the distribution and abundance of species. The most important factors in this respect are biotic ones, such as competition for light by plants.

Succession

We should not think of ecosystems as being permanent and stable, but as dynamic systems that are susceptible to change. This could happen, perhaps because of climate change – for example, a change in the annual pattern of rainfall.

In many cases, we can see that a particular ecosystem is undergoing a *progressive* change, known as **succession**. Succession can be

In a desert such as the Namib, in south-west Africa, water is in very short supply, making it very difficult for plants or animals to survive. Temperatures rise to very high levels during the day, then drop sharply at night.

In tropical rainforests, water is in abundant supply, there is plenty of light all the year round for plants, and the temperature range is relatively small.

defined as a directional change in an ecosystem over time. By definition, therefore, any ecosystem that is undergoing succession is an unstable one. If the succession begins on an area of completely bare ground, such as on a lava field after a volcanic eruption, or on ground uncovered by a retreating glacier, it is known as **primary succession**. If it begins on an area of ground that has been disturbed but where plants still remain – such as after the trees in a forest have been removed – then it is known as **secondary succession**. The different communities that appear at different stages of a succession are known as **seres**. The final community is known as the **climax community**.

Diversity and stability

In a succession, the early stages have a low species diversity and are very susceptible to change. The climax community has a much higher species diversity, and is much less susceptible to change. Is this true of ecosystems that are not simply different stages in a particular succession? Can it be generally stated that the greater the diversity within an ecosystem, the more stable it is? This topic has been the subject of great debate among ecologists for many years, and there still is no general agreement about it.

Some ecologists do suggest that the more complex an ecosystem is, the more stable it is. Such a view 'feels right' – most people would consider that a very diverse ecosystem would be better able to withstand a change than one in which only a few different species interacted. You can see how this might be true by thinking about relationships between predators and their prey in an ecosystem. In a complex ecosystem, food webs tend to have large numbers of links between many different organisms. A predator will probably have many different prey species. If one of these prey species disappears, this is unlikely to have any significant effect on the predator, as it can simply turn to another species as a food source. In a less complex system, however, a predator may have only a single prey species on which it depends. If that prey species disappears, then so does the predator, and the cumulative effects on other species within the ecosystem could be dramatic.

However, there is a strongly-supported view, based largely on mathematical models, that exactly the opposite is true. Supporters of this view say that the more complex an ecosystem is, with the more interactions between the different organisms in the community, then the more vulnerable it is to change.

Currently, researchers in this area suggest that it is not safe to generalise about the relationship between diversity and stability in an ecosystem. Ecosystems are complex and differ widely from one another. More experimental evidence is needed before we can safely say that high diversity *always* confers more stability on an ecosystem than low diversity.

- Factors that influence the distribution and abundance of organisms can be categorised as abiotic and biotic factors.

- Abiotic factors result from the non-living part of the ecosystem, such as temperature or water supply. Biotic factors result from the living parts of the ecosystem, such as competition and predation.

- Abiotic factors can vary greatly within a habitat, forming different microclimates which are important in determining the distribution of species within that habitat.

- Abiotic factors tend to act equally on large and small populations, and are said to be density-independent. Biotic factors tend to have a greater effect on large populations than on small populations, and are said to be density-dependent.

- In a hostile environment, abiotic factors are usually more important than biotic ones in determining abundance and distribution of organisms. In a non-hostile environment, biotic factors are more important.

- Diversity tends to be lower in hostile environments than in non-hostile environments.

- An ecosystem that is progressively changing is said to be undergoing succession. Succession usually involves a gradual change through time, in which a hostile environment with low species diversity becomes less hostile and develops greater diversity.

- There is some evidence that ecosystems with high diversity are more stable than those with low diversity, but other evidence goes against this view.

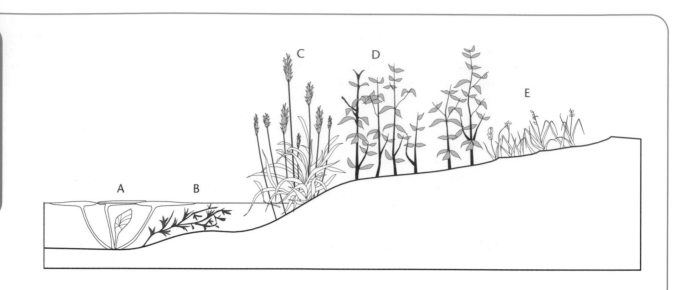

1 The drawing shows plants growing in and around a pond.

a With reference to the drawing, explain the meaning of the terms:
   i) community;
   ii) population. (3)

b Describe how you could use point quadrats to investigate the distribution of plants at the edge of a pond. (3)

NEAB BY05 March 1999 Q1

2 Blue tits are common British birds. Some aspects of the behaviour of blue tits at different times of the year are summarised below.

March–April	Adult birds establish breeding territories.
April–July	Breeding season. Eggs laid and young hatch. Adult birds collect food for their young from within their territories.
July–March	Birds form flocks which forage for food over a wide area.

a In a study of winter feeding flocks, 36 blue tits visiting a bird table were trapped, and before release each bird was marked by placing a small metal ring round one of its legs. The following day 43 blue tits were trapped. Of these, 21 were ringed. Estimate the size of the blue tit population visiting the bird table.

Show your working. (2)

b i) Give **two** reasons why the mark–release–recapture technique would not give a reliable estimate of the blue tit population in a wood between April and June. (2)

ii) Suggest how the population of adult blue tits in a wood might be estimated between April and June. (2)

NEAB BY05 March 1999 Q4

3

a An ecosystem can be described as a dynamic system involving interaction of biotic and abiotic components. Within an ecosystem populations of organisms occupy ecological niches.

Explain what is meant by the following terms:
   i) population; (1)
   ii) ecological niche. (2)

b The diagram shows the ranges of mean annual temperatures and precipitation (water falling as rain or snow) for six types of ecosystem.

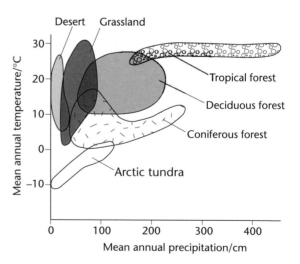

Arctic tundra is considered to be an extreme environment whereas tropical forest is physically less hostile to living organisms.

i) Explain how the information in the diagram supports this view. (1)

ii) Describe and explain the relative effect of abiotic factors on the diversity of organisms in the tundra and in the tropical forest. (2)

NEAB BY05 March 1998 Q2

4 Great tits are small British birds. During spring and summer, they are found in woodland where they nest in holes in trees. One of their main predators during this time is the weasel, a small mammal which is able to climb trees and enter nest holes. Weasels also prey on mice. The graphs show how three different factors affect the predation of great tits by weasels.

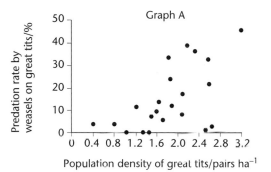

Graph A

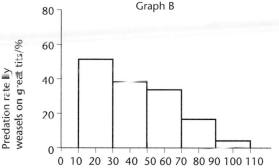

Graph B

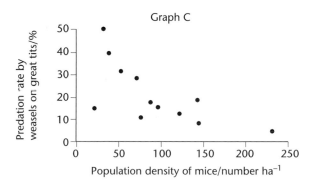

Graph C

a Describe how the mark–release–recapture method could be used to estimate the population of mice in the area being studied. What assumptions would you have to make in using this method? (6)

b Using information from the graphs, suggest how predation by weasels acts as a density-dependent factor controlling great tit population size. (4)

c Describe and explain the relationship between the percentage of great tits predated by weasels and the population density of mice shown in Graph C. (2)

NEAB BY05 June 1999 Q8

5

a Explain what is meant by an *ecological niche*. (2)

b Two species of beetle may be found in stored grain. The diagram shows the range of moisture content and temperature that each species can tolerate.

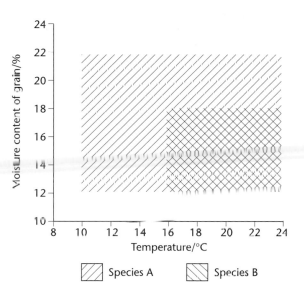

The temperature in different parts of a large grain store ranged from 14 °C to 20 °C. The moisture content of the grain was constant at 16%. Beetles of both species were introduced into the store. What would you expect to happen if:

i) species **A** were a more successful competitor than species **B**;

ii) species **B** were a more successful competitor than species **A**? (3)

NEAB BY05 June 1999 Q3

2 Effects of pollution on diversity

This chemical outfall is on its way to the River Mersey.

The activities of the growing human population on Earth are having large and wide-reaching effects on the distribution and abundance of other living organisms. In general, these effects tend to reduce biodiversity. One way in which this is happening is through **pollution**.

Although we all have an understanding of the meaning of the term 'pollution', it is not easy to find a definition that all scientists are satisfied with. One working definition that is widely used is *the addition to the environment of substances that are likely to cause harm to living organisms*. The harmful substances that are introduced are known as **pollutants**. However, this definition does not cover noise, heat or light pollution, because noise, heat and light cannot be said to be 'substances'.

Pollution may take place anywhere on Earth – in the air, on land, in fresh water or in the sea. In this chapter, we will concentrate on the pollution of water. We will consider some of the major sources and effects of pollution of both fresh water and the sea.

2.1 Monitoring pollution of aquatic ecosystems

In Britain, the organisation with official responsibility for monitoring pollution, including water pollution, is the Environment Agency. Many non-government organisations (NGOs) such as Greenpeace and Friends of the Earth keep a careful eye on pollution.

Different pollutants are released into water in different ways. Some are mainly from one location (a point source), for example an outlet of untreated sewage or runoff from a landfill site. Others are from sources that are spread over a larger area, such as agricultural run-off. Pollutants can enter the ecosystem all the time, or they may enter as isolated incidents, for example as a result of an industrial accident.

One way of finding out if water is polluted is to carry out chemical tests that indicate the presence of a particular substance. However, there are so many different substances that *could* be polluting a river, a lake or the sea, that it would be impossibly time-consuming and expensive to test for every possible pollutant. It is much more efficient to test for the *effects* of pollutants. Such tests include measuring **biochemical oxygen demand (BOD)**, looking for the presence or absence of **indicator species**, and the calculation of **diversity indices**. If these tests do indicate that the water is polluted, then tests for suspected individual pollutants can be carried out.

Biochemical oxygen demand

Some sources of water pollution may contain organic substances that act as nutrients for bacteria that live in rivers or the sea. Such pollutants include untreated (raw) sewage and run-off from food-processing factories. When such substances enter the water, the population sizes of the bacteria that feed on them are able to increase rapidly. These bacteria are aerobic – that is, they respire using oxygen. As their numbers increase, they use up more and more oxygen from the water. The concentration of dissolved oxygen therefore decreases, making it difficult or impossible for many other organisms to survive there.

Fertilisers containing nitrate, ammonium or phosphate ions have a similar effect. These fertilisers may be leached from farmland by rainfall, and run off into waterways. Here, however, the initial response is by algae that live in the water. The extra supply of these ions means that they grow faster than usual. An algal bloom may result, in which the population of algae becomes so large that it completely covers large areas of the water surface. These algae block the light from plants growing deeper in the water, so reducing their rate of photosynthesis. Eventually, the algae and plants die, providing large quantities of food for aerobic bacteria. The populations of these bacteria grow in the same way as when raw sewage enters the water, with the same eventual effect on dissolved oxygen concentrations.

This sequence of events is known as **eutrophication**. Eutrophication tends to result in decreased biodiversity in the water, because only organisms that are adapted to live in relatively low oxygen concentrations can survive. Organisms that require good

Algal bloom in shallow water at Rutland Water, a reservoir.

oxygen supplies – such as fish, mayfly larvae and many other invertebrates – either die or move to a less polluted place.

1a In Fig. 1, the point of minimum dissolved oxygen occurs below the point of discharge. Explain this observation.

b Why does the level of dissolved oxygen in the river eventually return to its original position?

One way of detecting whether these processes are happening is to measure the oxygen concentration in the water. This is quick and easy to do, using an electronic oxygen meter. A probe is placed in the water, and the meter gives an immediate digital read-out of oxygen concentration. More information can be obtained by measuring the BOD, the rate at which oxygen is being used up in a sample of water (Fig. 2). BOD is a measure of the rate of

Fig. 2 Measuring BOD

1 Completely fill two 250 cm^3 plastic flasks, A and B, with water sample. Try to close them under water to keep them free of air bubbles.

2 Record the oxygen concentration of flask A with an electronic meter.

3 Incubate flask B in the dark for five days at 20 °C. After the five days, record the oxygen concentration of flask B.

4 The 5-day BOD is the flask A oxygen concentration minus the flask B oxygen concentration.

Fig. 1 Effect of raw sewage on oxygen concentration

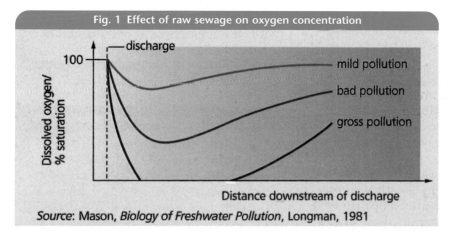

- discharge
- mild pollution
- bad pollution
- gross pollution

Dissolved oxygen/ % saturation

100

Distance downstream of discharge

Source: Mason, *Biology of Freshwater Pollution*, Longman, 1981

aerobic respiration of the microorganisms in the water, and therefore a measure of the size of their populations. A high BOD indicates pollution either with organic substances that directly stimulate the growth of bacterial populations, or with mineral ions (such as nitrate) that stimulate the growth of algae and plants whose remains then become a food source for microorganisms.

2a Suggest why it is important not to have any air bubbles in the flask at step 1 in Fig. 2.

b Suggest why the flasks are kept in the dark rather than in the light.

Indicator species

Different species of aquatic invertebrates have different requirements for the oxygen concentration of the water in which they live. So, a stretch of river that is heavily polluted and has a very high BOD (that is, dissolved oxygen is being rapidly used up) will contain a very different community of organisms from another stretch of the same river where there is no pollution. If you sample the invertebrates at various points in the river and make a record of which species are present, you can get a good idea of how polluted each area is. Species that are particularly useful for this, because they are fairly common yet restricted to living in water within a fairly narrow range of oxygen concentrations, are known as indicator species (Fig. 3).

Relatively few organisms are able to survive where oxygen concentration is very low. They include the sludge worm (*Tubifex*), blood worms (*Chironomus*) and rat-tailed maggots. All these invertebrates have special adaptations to help them to survive in these difficult conditions. Both *Tubifex* and *Chironomus* contain haemoglobin with a very high affinity for oxygen (much higher than that of human haemoglobin), so they can absorb oxygen even when the external concentrations are very low. Rat-tailed maggots have breathing tubes that they extend above the water surface, obtaining oxygen from the air.

Where oxygen concentration is high, many more invertebrates are able to survive. They include several different species of mayfly nymphs, caddis larvae and stonefly larvae. In water with intermediate oxygen concentrations, the freshwater shrimp *Gammarus* and several different species of leeches and snails may be found.

When using these species to indicate the level of pollution, each is given a **biotic index** number on a scale of 1 to 10. High numbers indicate that they require high oxygen levels, while low numbers indicate that they can tolerate very low oxygen levels. Table 1 shows the results of looking for

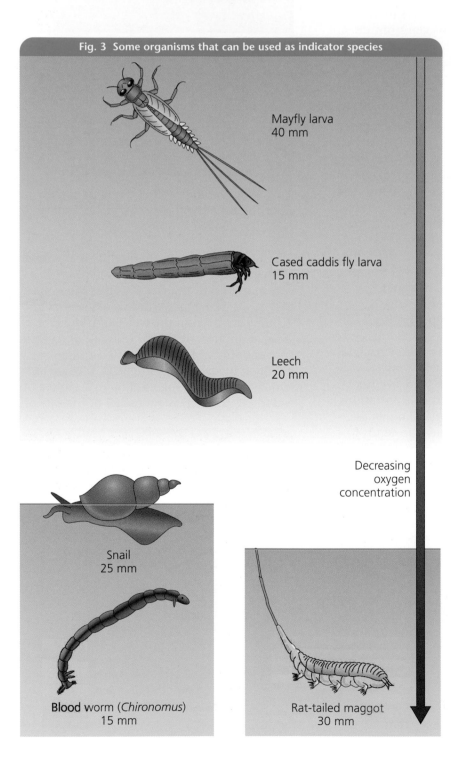

Fig. 3 Some organisms that can be used as indicator species

Mayfly larva
40 mm

Cased caddis fly larva
15 mm

Leech
20 mm

Snail
25 mm

Blood worm (*Chironomus*)
15 mm

Rat-tailed maggot
30 mm

Decreasing oxygen concentration

Table 1 Data from two sites						
Site 1	Biotic index	Number of individuals		Site 2	Biotic index	Number of individuals
Stonefly larvae				Mayfly larvae	4	8
Species 1	10	4		Snails	3	30
Species 2	10	7		Leeches		
Species 3	10	3		Species 1	3	1
Mayfly larvae				Species 2	3	2
Species 1	4	2		Fly larvae		
Species 2	10	7		Species 1	2	30
Cased caddis larvae				Species 2	2	65
With stones	10	2		Worms	1	120
With leaves	7	1				
Freshwater shrimp	6	35				
Leeches						
Species 1	3	11				
Species 2	3	3				
Snails						
Species 1	3	45				
Species 2	3	16				

indicator species in two different rivers. At Site 1, there are several organisms with the highest possible biotic index (10), which shows that this site has plenty of oxygen in the water and therefore is not polluted with organic effluents or fertilisers. At Site 2, there is no organism with a biotic index above 4. This indicates that there is significant pollution here. The next step would be to analyse a sample of water from this site, to try to determine exactly what pollution is causing the low oxygen concentration.

3 Although organisms with a biotic index of 1 or 2 are able to survive in water where oxygen concentrations are very low, they can also survive in well-oxygenated water. Suggest why no organisms with a biotic index below 3 are found at Site 1.

Gammarus, the freshwater shrimp, has a biotic index of 6 and is found at Site 1.

Diversity indices

The results from surveys such as those shown in Table 1 can be used to calculate a diversity index. Simpson's Diversity Index (p. 13) is sometimes used in this situation. Another commonly used index is the **Margalef Index**, which is calculated from the formula:

$$I = \frac{S - 1}{\log N}$$

Where
I = Margalef Index
S = number of species
N = number of individuals of each species.

A high diversity index indicates an unpolluted river with high oxygen concentration. A low diversity index is very suggestive of pollution, as it is likely to be the cause of low oxygen concentration.

The advantages of using diversity indices rather than biotic indices include:

- species and types need only be distinguished from one another so that you can count them – they do not need to be actually identified;

- no information on the oxygen tolerance of each species is required.

4a Calculate the Margalef Index for each of the two sites in Table 1.

b Comment on the differences between the two sites.

- Regular sampling of water can be used to monitor changes in its living and non-living contents and indicate the presence of any pollution.

- Oxygen is the most important variable in water quality.

- Low oxygen concentrations indicate pollution with organic substances that provide nutrients for bacteria, or with inorganic ions that provide nutrients for algae and plants.

- Biochemical oxygen demand is a measure of the rate at which oxygen is used. A high BOD indicates high populations of aerobic bacteria, a sign of pollution.

- The presence and absence of indicator species provides a measure of water quality.

- Diversity indices can be used to assess water quality.

2.2 Heavy metal ions

Heavy metals have high relative atomic masses, for example mercury and lead. Such metals can be highly toxic to living organisms, because they act as enzyme inhibitors. They tend to bind with enzyme molecules at a place other than their active site, so they are non-competitive inhibitors. Enzymes are therefore permanently prevented from catalysing their specific reactions, resulting in all sorts of unpleasant physiological symptoms, and sometimes even death.

	Table 2 Some examples of heavy metal pollutants		
Heavy metal	**Major sources**	**Biological effects**	**Symptoms**
Lead (Pb)	Leaded petrol; lead in old water pipes or solder; lead pigments in paints	Inhibition of the synthesis of proteins containing haem groups, such as haemoglobin and cytochromes; binds to sulphur-containing side chains on the amino acid cysteine, thus affecting many types of protein	*Acute poisoning*: intestinal cramps, kidney failure, sterility, irreversible brain damage *Chronic exposure*: anaemia, learning difficulties
Mercury (Hg)	Factories manufacturing some types of electrical goods; the chloralkali industry (uses mercury as an electrode in the production of NaOH and Cl_2 from NaCl); dental fillings	Binds with and inhibits many types of enzyme	Extensive damage to the nervous system, resulting in neurological disorders
Cadmium (Cd)	Electroplating; pigments in paints; zinc smelting (cadmium often contaminates zinc ores); cigarette smoke	Blocks sulphur-containing groups in cysteine, so affecting many proteins including enzymes; interferes with metabolic pathways involving copper or zinc Readily taken up by plants from soil water and is very toxic to them	Consumption of plants containing cadmium by humans causes itai-itai (disease in which bones become very fragile); may cause prostate cancer; reduces filtration ability of glomeruli in kidneys

Mercury pollution in Minamata Bay

and also their cats, ate considerable quantities of seafood obtained from the polluted bay. In 1953, the cats began to show strange neurological symptoms, and before long all the cats had died. By 1956, so many of the local people had become ill that doctors at last began to realise that something strange was going on.

The symptoms of poisoning with methyl mercury are very unpleasant. Victims salivate heavily, and suffer convulsions and staggering. Children were born with severe mental retardation and with cerebral palsy. But it was 10 years before anyone publicly acknowledged that these problems were caused by mercury pollution. At Minamata Bay, at least 798 people either died or suffered permanent damage to their central nervous system.

From 1932 to 1970, a factory in Japan manufactured acetaldehyde. Part of this process involved the use of mercury, Hg. Although the effluent from the factory was not monitored at the time, it is now estimated that approximately 600 tonnes of methyl mercury were discharged into the sea at Minamata Bay.

Mercury is highly toxic to almost all living organisms. And methyl mercury, CH_3Hg, is particularly dangerous because it is soluble in lipids. In Minamata Bay, therefore, it was able to enter the cells of any aquatic organisms that came into contact with or ingested the polluted sea water.

Organisms near the bottom of the food chain, such as phytoplankton and zooplankton, absorbed the methyl mercury. It was not broken down in their bodies, but remained there, accumulating especially in lipid-rich tissues. When other organisms such as shellfish and fish fed on the plankton, the methyl mercury entered their bodies. The more plankton they ate, the more methyl mercury accumulated within them. They soon came to contain even higher concentrations of methyl mercury than the plankton. Organisms higher up the food chain, feeding on the shellfish and fish, built up even higher concentrations of methyl mercury in their bodies. This process, in which a pollutant becomes increasingly concentrated as it passes along a food chain, is known as **bioaccumulation**.

One species that fed on the shellfish and the fish was humans. Fishermen and their families,

The illness suffered by the children who were born with damaged brains and bodies became known as Minamata Disease.

1 a Explain why substances that are lipid-soluble are able to enter cells more easily than substances that do not dissolve in lipids.

b Suggest how the fact that this pollution occurred in a bay, rather than a more open area of coastline, may have affected the severity of the problems suffered by the local population.

c Explain why, even when the source of the mercury pollution was stopped, its effects would take a long time to disappear from the community of marine animals living in Minamata Bay.

Assessing toxicity

The toxicity of a heavy metal depends on a number of factors, especially:

- whether it is adsorbed to the substrate or is free in solution;

- its persistence;

- how much and for how long an organism has been exposed to it;

- how quickly it enters an organism's cells;

- any bioaccumulation that occurs.

Measurements of the toxicity of a substance for particular species are usually found by exposing laboratory or test populations to different amounts of the substance.

Several different populations are each exposed to a different dose of the substance, and a graph is drawn of the percentage of the population that is killed against the amount of the chemical they were given. From this, the amount of the substance that kills 50% of the population can be deduced, and this is known as the **LD_{50}** (LD stands for lethal dose). The lower the LD_{50} for a substance, the more toxic it is to that particular species.

In water, it is the *concentration* of the substance that is most relevant, and in this case the concentration of the substance that kills 50% of the population is measured. This is known as the **LC_{50}** for that substance for that species.

The application of laboratory-derived measures, such as LC_{50} and LD_{50}, to wild populations is increasingly being questioned by ecologists. These measures often fail to take account of environmental conditions such as water pH, oxygen levels, temperature, and other effects produced by combinations of many factors, which can modify toxic effects. Sometimes, these effects can work together to make things even worse than would be expected by simply totalling up the effects. This is known as **synergism**. In other cases, the effect of one pollutant may actually reduce the effects of another. This is known as **antagonism**.

Table 3 LD_{50} of some heavy metals			
	Copper	**Cadmium**	**Zinc**
Stone loach	0.26	2.0	2.5
	(63)	(54)	(5)
Rainbow trout	0.28	0.017	4.6
	(119)	(5.5)	(5)

Exposure time in days is in brackets.

Source: Solbe and Cooper, *Water Resources*, Vol 10, pp. 523–527, 1976

5 Compare the degree of tolerance in the two species of fish in Table 3.

KEY FACTS

- Heavy metals are toxic to living organisms because they bind with enzymes at a position other than the active site, therefore acting as non-competitive inhibitors.

- Heavy metals can get into waterways in effluent from some industrial processes.

- Heavy metals are elements; they are not broken down. They can bioaccumulate; that is, become more concentrated in the tissues of living organisms further along a food chain.

- The toxicity of heavy metals on living organisms can be measured in the laboratory as their LC_{50} or LD_{50} – that is, the concentration or dose that kills 50% of individuals of a particular species in a certain time.

- Aquatic organisms differ in their sensitivity to heavy metal pollutants.

2.3 Acid rain

Rain is naturally slightly acidic due to the presence of carbon dioxide, CO_2. Carbon dioxide and water combine to form carbonic acid, with a pH of 5.65. However, **acid rain** can be much more acidic than this. Acid rain is usually defined as any precipitation (not only rain, but also snow, sleet and hail) that has a pH below 5.6.

Acid rain first became a public concern in the post-war 'smogs' that plagued London and other major industrial cities. The worst example in London occurred in 1953 when the pH of the smog caused by factory smoke and a week-long fog fell to 1.6. This was responsible for the deaths of 4000 people who suffered from breathing difficulties and respiratory diseases. In the early 1970s, Sweden complained that the acidity of rain falling in southern Scandinavia had greatly increased since the 1950s, and that this was due to pollutants from countries such as Britain.

Sources of acid rain

The acidic level of rain can be influenced by the effect of naturally occurring chemicals and processes (Fig. 4). Rain becomes acidic when certain gases rise into the atmosphere, and then react with water in the droplets that make up clouds. The gases that are responsible for acidification are:

- sulphur dioxide, SO_2;
- the various oxides of nitrogen
  - nitrous oxide, N_2O
  - nitric oxide, NO
  - nitrogen dioxide, NO_2.

The different nitrogen oxides are collectively known as NO_x.

Sulphur dioxide and nitrogen oxides are emitted naturally from active volcanoes. They are also emitted from the burning of fossil fuels.

Sulphur dioxide is emitted when fossil fuels that contain sulphur compounds are burnt. Coal tends to contain a lot of these compounds, whereas diesel and petrol contain hardly any. Motor vehicle exhausts, therefore, do *not* contribute significantly to sulphur dioxide emissions. Most sulphur dioxide comes from coal-burning power stations, and from metal-smelting industries. Nitrogen oxides are formed in car engines, when nitrogen from the air combines with oxygen. The nitrogen does *not* come from the fuel.

These oxides are all gases, and they can be carried high into the air above the source that emits them. Here, they oxidise, and then combine with water, forming sulphuric acid, H_2SO_4 and nitric acid, HNO_3. Droplets of water containing these acids can be carried hundreds of miles in clouds, eventually falling as acid rain in countries far from their original sources.

Effects of acid rain

Acid rain falling onto plants can be harmful to them. It weakens trees and other plants, making them more susceptible to other stresses, such as drought. However, the effects of acid rain can spread far more widely than the immediate area where it falls. It percolates into the soil, and then eventually flows into waterways.

The severity of the effects of acid rain varies considerably between areas with different kinds of underlying rock. In limestone areas, the calcium carbonate in the

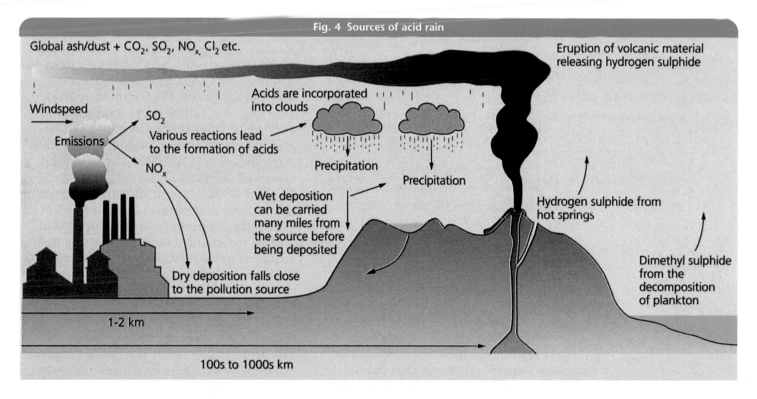

Fig. 4 Sources of acid rain

Global ash/dust + CO_2, SO_2, NO_x, Cl_2 etc.

Eruption of volcanic material releasing hydrogen sulphide

Windspeed

Emissions

SO_2

NO_x

Various reactions lead to the formation of acids

Acids are incorporated into clouds

Precipitation

Precipitation

Wet deposition can be carried many miles from the source before being deposited

Dry deposition falls close to the pollution source

Hydrogen sulphide from hot springs

Dimethyl sulphide from the decomposition of plankton

1-2 km

100s to 1000s km

soil reacts with and neutralises the acids in the rain falling onto them. In such areas, acid rain does little harm to living organisms – although it does speed up the erosion of the limestone by dissolving it. In regions where the underlying rocks do not contain calcium carbonate, there is nothing to neutralise the acidity of the rain, and effects in these areas are much greater.

Effects on aquatic organisms

In non-limestone areas, as the acid rain water spreads through the soil, various ions dissolve in it that would not do so if the water had a higher pH. These include aluminium, lead, and cadmium. These ions are washed into waterways, where they can have harmful effects on aquatic organisms. Lead and cadmium are very toxic to living organisms (Table 2, p. 26). Aluminium ions are particularly harmful to young fish where they:

- reduce the efficiency of oxygen uptake by haemoglobin;

- increase the amount of mucus on fish gills, which reduces the efficiency of gas exchange;

- reduce the action of the enzyme responsible for dissolving the egg membrane of the larval stages of fish such as salmon and trout, which prevents them hatching.

Another problem is that water with a low pH tends to contain fewer calcium ions than water with a relatively high pH. Many aquatic organisms make shells of calcium carbonate, and if they cannot obtain enough calcium from the water, then they cannot grow and reproduce. In Norwegian lakes, the number of

species of molluscs and crustaceans decreases markedly with decreasing pH. Both of these types of organism require calcium to produce their shells and exoskeletons. In one study, it was found that birds such as dippers feeding on these invertebrates in acidified waters produced thin-shelled eggs that did not hatch.

Low pH can also cause phosphate ions to precipitate out of water. Thus, phosphate is no longer available for aquatic plants to absorb. As phosphate is an essential plant nutrient, phytoplankton and other plants die, so there is less food for herbivores, which affects the whole of the food chain.

Aquatic organisms vary widely in their tolerance to acidity, and so can be used as indicator species (Fig. 5).

6a Looking at Fig. 5, identify two species that are indicators of high pH.

b Identify two species that are indicators of low pH.

Reducing the incidence of acid rain

In western Europe and in North America, the problem of acid rain is being tackled very successfully. Emissions that cause acid rain began to decrease in North America in the early 1970s, and in Europe in the 1960s. In Europe, for example, the average concentration of sulphate (SO_4^{2-}) ions in rain water decreased from 2.4 mg dm^{-3} in 1985 to 1.5 mg dm^{-3} in 1996. However, this is not the case throughout the world, and acid rain is still a major problem in some parts of Asia, for example.

The measures that have led to this improvement in Europe and North America include:

- the use of catalytic converters on car exhausts; these catalyse the conversion of nitrogen oxides to harmless nitrogen and oxygen, which are then emitted in the exhaust gases;

- the use of 'scrubbers' in coal-burning power stations; the waste gases that contain sulphur dioxide are passed through a spray of lime and water, which reacts with and removes the sulphur.

Even when acid rain is no longer falling, it can take a very long time for aquatic ecosystems to recover from its effects. It will take many years for the effects of acid rain on the soil, and therefore on the ions that are washed into lakes and rivers, to be reversed.

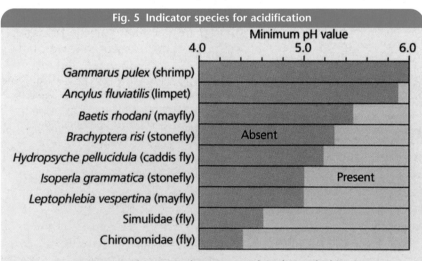

Fig. 5 Indicator species for acidification

Source: Cadogan and Best, *Environment and Ecology*, Blackie, 1992

- Acid rain is precipitation with a pH lower than 5.6.

- Acid rain is formed after sulphur dioxide and nitrogen oxides are released into the air. They are oxidised and react with water in the air, forming sulphuric acid and nitric acid.

- Acid rain may fall hundreds of miles from the place where the gases were emitted.

- Acid rain washes heavy metal ions out of soil and into waterways; these ions may harm many species of aquatic organisms.

- Acidified water contains fewer calcium ions, and organisms that require these to make exoskeletons or shells may not be able to grow or reproduce.

- Acid rain results in the precipitation of phosphate ions, which therefore become unavailable to producers such as phytoplankton and plants. This reduces the food supply at the bottom of food chains.

- Aquatic species differ in their sensitivity to the effects of acid rain, and so can be used as indicators.

2.4 Oil pollution

Major oil pollution events – such as when a tanker is wrecked and spills its load – make headline news. We see vivid pictures of black, thick oil lying on the surface of the sea, collecting on beaches and coating seabirds. In fact, oil pollution is probably less harmful in terms of the long-term effects than many other sources of pollution that rarely make the headlines. Nevertheless, the effects of oil pollution are very unpleasant, and they deservedly attract the attention of the media and of environmentally aware individuals and organisations.

Sources of oil pollution

Huge oil tankers carry enormous volumes of oil all around the world. Much of this oil is **crude oil** – that is, oil as it comes out of the ground, before it has been separated by fractional distillation into its various components such as petrol, kerosene and bitumen. Crude oil is a mixture of many different hydrocarbons, all of which are potentially harmful to living things, and are insoluble in water.

If an oil tanker is wrecked, then its cargo usually spills into the sea. The lighter components float on the surface, because they are less dense than water. The heavier components may sink to the bottom, especially if the sea is rough, which breaks up the slick and helps the oil to mix with the water.

Oil pollution can also occur from under-sea oil wells. When Iraq occupied Kuwait at the beginning of the Gulf War in 1991, Kuwait's oil wells in the Arabian Gulf were deliberately damaged, releasing huge amounts of oil into the sea. Sometimes, accidents at oil rigs occur, such as the IXTOC 1 oil platform blow-out in the Gulf of Mexico in 1979.

Even much smaller-scale oil spillages can be harmful to living things. Oil slowly seeping into harbours from moored boats, or into effluent from a factory, may never build up into very high concentrations but over long periods of time its effects may be considerable. On an even smaller scale, one person carelessly throwing away old engine oil into a drain may pollute a nearby small stream so badly that almost every living thing in it is destroyed.

Effects of oil pollution on aquatic organisms

Oil floating on the water surface can harm living organisms in many ways. Sea birds resting on the water get oil on their feathers, which is impossible for them to clean off. Feathers act as excellent heat insulation for birds because they trap air between them, but when they are oiled very little air is trapped, and the bird's body rapidly loses heat. Oiled birds often cannot fly, because their wing feathers cannot spread out to support them in the air; they are also less buoyant. Attempts to clean themselves lead to ingestion of oil, which contains toxic substances, so the birds may be poisoned. Many oiled sea birds are found along seashores after an oil spill. People may try to clean their feathers using detergents before releasing them back into the wild, but follow-up studies show that few of these birds survive for very long after this ordeal, perhaps dying as a result of ingesting oil, or of shock.

The oil blocks light from passing into the sea water, so that phytoplankton cannot photosynthesise. This loss of productivity has effects right through the food chain.

Toxic compounds in oil can affect almost any aquatic organism. Those that live on seashores are especially vulnerable, because oil is often washed onto the shore and remains there. Sessile organisms such as limpets and sea anemones may become coated with a layer of oil, which usually kills them. The oil can also block the filter-feeding mechanisms of animals such as mussels and tube worms.

CASE STUDY

The *Amoco Cadiz* oil spill

In mid-March 1978, the supertanker *Amoco Cadiz* was carrying 223 000 tonnes of crude oil from Iran around the coast of north-eastern France. During the night of 16–17 March, the ship was wrecked in heavy weather. It sank only 2.8 km from the coast of Brittany. All of its cargo was lost into the sea.

The crude oil that the *Amoco Cadiz* was carrying was made up of light fractions, which floated on the sea water. About 40% was volatile compounds that easily evaporate, and these were lost to the air within a few days. However, 30% was made up of highly toxic aromatic hydrocarbons.

The strong winds and rough seas helped the oil to spread quickly. For the next two weeks, westerly winds blew the oil onto the shoreline of Brittany. A 360 km length of coastline – a mix of rocky shores, sandy beaches, salt marshes and estuaries – became covered with oil. Out at sea, heavy weather helped some of the oil to disperse into the water, which although it did not get rid of it did help to reduce its effects.

Many animals living along the shoreline were killed. Students from the Université de Bretagne Occidental estimated that there were 10^6 dead heart urchins, 7.5×10^6 dead cockles and 7.0×10^6 other dead bivalves at just one stretch of sandy shore at St Efflam. On rocky shores, animals that lived beneath boulders seemed to be the most affected, perhaps because oil tended to accumulate there. It was also estimated that up to 20 000 seabirds died, as well as numerous fish. Seaweeds, on the other hand, did not seem to be too badly affected.

There were also delayed effects on many species. The reproductive abilities of plaice, mullet and eels were greatly reduced. In the case of the eels, investigation showed that oocytes in their ovaries had completely degenerated soon after their exposure to the oil. Some fish also seemed to become more susceptible to diseases, such as fin rot disease in plaice, sole and mullet.

Nevertheless, there is little evidence that any animal or plant species was completely wiped out in the polluted area. This should mean that, given time, their populations will gradually recover. Many were well on their way to doing this by the mid-1980s, less than 10 years after the *Amoco Cadiz* was wrecked. For example, the initial increases in fin rot disease in fish rapidly declined. But in some places, particularly the sandy shores and estuaries, the effects are taking a very long time to be reversed. On the sandy beach at St Efflam, there were still no heart urchins present in 1982. No-one yet knows whether these ecosystems will completely return to their state before the oil spill.

1 Oil is biodegradable, so if left alone it will eventually break down and disappear. However, after disasters such as the *Amoco Cadiz* oil spill, people naturally want to clean up the oil as quickly as possible. Suggest possible disadvantages of each of the following methods of doing this:

a spraying detergent onto beaches to help to disperse the oil

b setting light to the oil slick on the water.

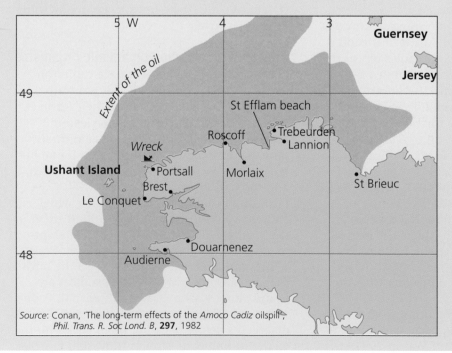

Source: Conan, 'The long-term effects of the *Amoco Cadiz* oilspill', *Phil. Trans. R. Soc. Lond. B*, **297**, 1982

KEY FACTS

- Oil is not soluble, so oil spilled into fresh or salt water tends to float on the surface or sink to the bottom.

- Surface oil slicks can clog birds' feathers, damaging their heat insulation properties, and making it difficult for the birds to float or to fly.

- Crude oil contains many toxic substances, which can kill birds, fish and many invertebrates.

- An oil slick stops light penetrating into the water, thus preventing photosynthesis and upsetting food webs.

EXAMINATION QUESTIONS

1 During the first half of the 20th century the River Thames became heavily polluted. One of the most important sources of pollution was sewage. In the mid 1960s serious efforts were started to reduce this pollution. Two major sewage works were improved or extended, one in 1964 and the other in 1976. As a result of this, the concentration of dissolved oxygen In the River Thames increased.

a Explain the relationship between improvements in sewage treatment and the concentration of dissolved oxygen in the River Thames. (4)

b Since the improvement in sewage treatment, there have been increases in both the number of fish and the number of different species of fish.

Suggest and explain two reasons for the correlation between increased oxygen concentrations and the number of different species of fish. (4)

NEAB BY05 February 1997 Q5

2 A *diversity index* can be used to compare the level of pollution at different places along a stream. It may be calculated from the number of small animals in samples collected in the stream. These animals cling to plants or stones, or live on the bed of the stream.

a i) Suggest two techniques which could be used to capture the small animals in order to calculate the index. (2)

ii) Give two precautions which must be taken in order to make a valid comparison of the diversity of organisms at different places along the stream. (2)

b Suggest one factor that could affect the concentration of oxygen in a stream and explain how it would have its effect. (2)

NEAB BY05 March 1998 Q1

3 Explain how each of the following may result in damage to an aquatic ecosystem:

a Spillage of crude oil. (3)

b Emission of sulphur dioxide into the atmosphere. (3)

NEAB BY05 March 2

4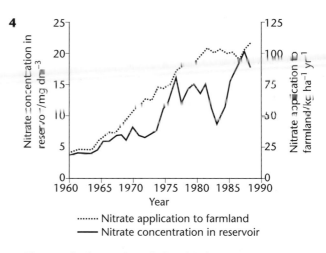

.... Nitrate application to farmland
—— Nitrate concentration in reservoir

a The graph shows the relationship between nitrate application to farmland and the concentration of nitrate in a nearby reservoir.

i) Explain why there was an overall increase in the concentration of nitrate in the reservoir between 1960 and 1990. (1)

ii) Suggest one explanation for the large fall in nitrate concentration in the reservoir between 1982 and 1984. (2)

b Explain why there is concern at the amount of nitrates being leaked into rivers, lakes and reservoirs. (4)

NEAB BY05 June 1999 Q8

3 Adaptations for survival

Every species of living organism is able to live successfully only in a particular range of environmental conditions; each species is adapted to its habitat.

Each species has evolved adaptations that increase its chances of survival and reproduction within a particular type of habitat. These adaptations may be:

- structural – to do with the size, shape and structure of the body;
- physiological – to do with the way the body works;
- behavioural.

Many adaptations involve two or more of these categories. For example, the structure of a desert mouse's kidneys is linked with the way that they function, and the structure of the salt bush's leaves affect the way that it deals with excess salt in its environment. Similarly, behavioural adaptations are often linked closely with structural or physiological ones.

3.1 Structural adaptation

Structural adaptations are often the most obvious, when we look at an animal or plant and think about how it may be adapted for its particular niche in its particular habitat. It is easy to see how a giraffe's long neck adapts it for feeding on leaves on tall trees, or how a seal's streamlined body adapts it for swimming through water. Here, we will concentrate on just two examples of structural adaptation – adaptations of animals for living in hot or cold climates, and adaptations of plants for living in areas where water is in short supply.

Size and shape of animals in hot and cold climates

Mammals
Mammals are **endothermic** organisms. They are able to maintain their body temperature well above the temperature of their environment, by generating heat inside their bodies. The heat is produced by respiration, which takes place in every cell in the body. Humans, for example, keep their body temperature at around 37 °C, even when the environmental temperature is much lower than this.

Heat is lost from an animal through its body surface. The greater the difference in temperature between the warm body and its cooler surroundings, the faster the rate of heat loss. Some is lost as infrared radiation from the blood in the capillaries in the skin, and some is lost in convection currents – air next to a warm animal's skin warms up, becomes less dense and rises away from the animal's body. Heat is also lost by sweating, because when the water in sweat evaporates it absorbs large amounts of heat energy as the liquid water turns to vapour.

To maintain a relatively constant internal body temperature, mammals must keep a balance between heat production inside their bodies, and heat loss from their body surface. In very cold conditions, they need a very high rate of heat production, in order to offset the high heat losses.

The rate at which heat can be *produced* is affected by the quantity of respiring cells. The bigger the volume of the animal, the more cells there are and the more heat it can produce. But the rate at which heat is *lost* is affected by the area of the animal in contact with its environment. Thus, rate of heat production is proportional to volume, while rate of heat loss is proportional to surface area.

Large animals have a smaller surface area to volume ratio than small animals. So it is much easier for a large animal to keep its body temperature above that of its surroundings than it is for a small animal. It is not surprising, therefore, to find that mammals that live in very cold climates tend to be larger than their close relatives that live in warm climates. Related animals in temperate climates are intermediate in size. Moreover, mammals that live in cold climates tend to have rounded bodies with thick layers of insulating fat beneath the skin. They also tend to have small ears – big ears would present a large surface area through which heat could be lost.

Reptiles

Reptiles do not generate large amounts of heat inside their bodies, so they are not endothermic. They are **ectothermic** animals, meaning that their body heat is absorbed from their environment. Reptiles use behavioural methods to regulate their temperature. At night, when temperature drops, the body temperature of the reptile also drops. This reduces its metabolic rate and it becomes inactive. In the morning, as temperatures rise, the reptile may bask in the sun to warm up, so increasing its metabolic activity.

Body features that maximise the rate at which heat can be absorbed by basking are therefore an advantage to some species. For example, adders that live in northern Europe beyond the Arctic Circle tend to be black, rather than with zig-zag patterning. Black is better at absorbing heat than lighter colours, so these black snakes warm up faster and become active earlier in the day than those with zig-zags. In an area like this, it could be useful to have a *small* body with a large surface area to volume ratio, as this increases the rate at which heat is absorbed and distributed to body cells. However, once the

Polar bears are the largest of all bears, reaching lengths of up to 2.5 m.

Sun bears, which live in south-east Asia, have a maximum size of 1.4 m.

heat has been absorbed then it becomes advantageous to have a *large* body, as this has a lower surface area to volume ratio and is better able to retain the heat over longer periods of time. These conflicting advantages and disadvantages mean that there is no general pattern of reptile size and shape in different climates. However, all the largest reptiles – for example crocodiles, Komodo dragons (very large lizards that live in Indonesia) and big snakes such as pythons and anacondas – live in countries with warm climates.

1 In northern Sweden, the black forms of the adder grow to a much larger size than those with the lighter, zig-zag patterning. Suggest a reason for this.

Desert conditions and plants

Plants, like all organisms, require water for their survival. Terrestrial plants take up water by osmosis through their root hairs – a passive process in which water diffuses down a water potential gradient from the soil into the root hair cells. The water is then transported through the plant in xylem vessels. Some of the water is used for photosynthesis, and some is retained in the plant within cells as they grow, but the vast majority is lost as water vapour. Most of this loss of water vapour, known as transpiration, takes place from the leaves, largely through the stomata.

In order to retain sufficient water in their cells, plants must balance the rate at which water enters through the root hairs against the rate at which it is lost from the leaves. If water is in abundant supply, this is no problem. But plants that can survive where water is scarce, such as in deserts, have evolved a number of adaptations to reduce the rate of water loss. Such plants are known as **xerophytes**.

Many xerophytes, for example the desert-living succulent *Aloe*, have leaves with especially thick, waxy cuticles that effectively waterproof them(Fig. 1). Waxy scales also help to reflect radiation from the sun, so reducing its heating effect during the day.

Leaves may also be covered with hairs, which effectively trap a layer of humid air next to the leaf surface. This decreases the diffusion gradient for water vapour between the inside and outside of the leaf, so reducing transpiration. Marram grass, *Ammophila arenaria*, which grows on sand dunes near to the sea, is able to roll up its leaves in dry conditions, with the stomata on the inside (Fig. 2).

Many xerophytes have swollen leaves, containing tissues that store water. This also has the effect of reducing the surface area to volume ratio, decreasing the area from which loss of water vapour can occur. Other xerophytes use their thickened, photosynthetic stems to store water, and may have leaves reduced to nothing more than small spines. The prickly pear cactus, *Opuntia* sp., is an example of such a plant. A bonus of such an arrangement is that the spines deter thirsty animals from eating the juicy plant tissues.

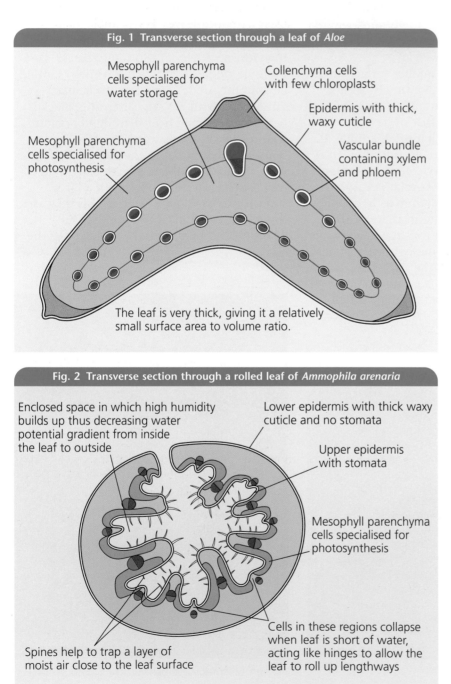

Fig. 1 Transverse section through a leaf of *Aloe*

Mesophyll parenchyma cells specialised for water storage

Collenchyma cells with few chloroplasts

Epidermis with thick, waxy cuticle

Mesophyll parenchyma cells specialised for photosynthesis

Vascular bundle containing xylem and phloem

The leaf is very thick, giving it a relatively small surface area to volume ratio.

Fig. 2 Transverse section through a rolled leaf of *Ammophila arenaria*

Enclosed space in which high humidity builds up thus decreasing water potential gradient from inside the leaf to outside

Lower epidermis with thick waxy cuticle and no stomata

Upper epidermis with stomata

Mesophyll parenchyma cells specialised for photosynthesis

Cells in these regions collapse when leaf is short of water, acting like hinges to allow the leaf to roll up lengthways

Spines help to trap a layer of moist air close to the leaf surface

CASE STUDY   Halophytes

Mangrove trees such as *Brugelera gymnorrhiza* grow on sea shores where they are flooded by salt water twice a day. Mangroves are able to stop salt from being taken up into their xylem vessels.

Halophytes are specialised xerophytes that live in salty conditions. In salt marshes, where soil contains high concentrations of salt, the dissolved salt lowers the water potential of the soil solution. Often, this water potential is lower than the water potential inside the root hairs of most plants. In these circumstances, water tends to diffuse *out* of the root hair cells rather than into them. The plants not only cannot absorb water, but may actually lose it by osmosis from their roots. Some halophytes solve this problem by absorbing the salts into their root hairs, which keeps their water potential below that of the soil solution. They deal with the salts by storing them in vacuoles, or by excreting them. The saltbush, *Atriplex*, for example, has special glands that concentrate salt and store it inside hundreds of tiny bladders on its leaves. Eventually, the bladders burst and the salt is washed away by rain.

Like desert-living plants, halophytes also need to conserve water by reducing water losses from their leaves. For example, *Atriplex hastata* has stomata that are sunken into deep pits.

Atriplex spongiosa lives in semi-arid and salty conditions in Australia.

1 Suggest why there is currently great interest in breeding varieties of agricultural plants that have halophytic adaptations.

KEY FACTS

- Endothermic animals such as mammals generate heat within their bodies.

- The rate at which animals can produce heat is proportional to their volume; the rate at which they lose it is proportional to their surface area.

- In cold climates, mammals with a small surface area to volume ratio are better able to maintain their internal body temperature than mammals with a large surface area to volume ratio.

- Ectothermic animals such as reptiles obtain body heat from their environment.

- For reptiles, there is no general relationship between climate and body size, although all of the largest reptiles do live in warm climates.

- Plants that live in places where water is in short supply are called xerophytes. They have adaptations that reduce the rate of water loss. These include water storage tissues, low surface area to volume ratios, especially thick cuticles, reduced leaf area and sunken stomata.

- Plant living in salty conditions are called halophytes. Besides adaptations to reduce water loss, they may also have ways of actively removing salt from their tissues.

3.2 Physiological adaptation

Structural and physiological adaptations often go hand in hand. This is certainly true of the adaptations of small desert-living rodents, and adaptations of plants for maximising photosynthesis in hot climates.

Water balance in desert rodents

Rodents are mammals that belong to the order Rodentia – the most successful group of mammals in terms of number of species, and the range of environments in which they are able to live. They include rats, mice, squirrels, guinea pigs, hamsters, porcupines, beavers and lemmings. The easiest way to tell if a mammal is a rodent is to look at its teeth – rodents always have a long pair of chisel-like incisor teeth projecting from the top and bottom jaws at the front of the mouth.

The main problem for animals that live in deserts is availability of water. Few desert rodents need to drink water. They obtain all the water they need in the food that they eat, and as a product of respiration inside their cells. Some, such as *Calomys musculinus*, which lives in deserts in Argentina, do this on a diet that consists almost entirely of dry seeds.

Such small inputs of water are sufficient only if water loss is equally small. Desert rodents have adaptations that greatly reduce water loss from their bodies. All mammals lose water in the air they breathe out, and in their urine. Moreover, mammals are endotherms; many rely on sweating to help to keep their body temperature below that of the environment. Desert rodents cannot afford to lose water by sweating, and must find other ways of keeping cool. Many spend the hot, dry days sleeping in cooler, more humid burrows deep in the soil. They become active at night when the temperature has dropped. This also helps to reduce water loss from the lungs.

2 Explain how remaining in a burrow helps to reduce water loss from the lungs.

The kidneys of desert rodents are structurally and physiologically adapted to keep the amount of water lost in urine to a minimum. All mammals, including humans, are capable of excreting urine that is more concentrated than their blood. This is achieved by the loops of Henle, which dip into the medulla of the kidney (Fig. 3). These loops allow a high concentration of sodium and chloride ions to build up in the tissues surrounding them. They act as counter-current multipliers; and the longer the loops, the higher the salt concentration that can build up. As fluid nears the end of the nephron, passing through the collecting ducts, it runs through this area of highly-concentrated tissue fluid. Water moves out of the fluid in the collecting ducts by osmosis – and the greater the concentration gradient for this, the more water leaves. The result is a highly concentrated urine.

Hystrix africaeaustralis, Cape porcupine

Xerus princeps, Kaokoveld ground squirrel

Allactaga hotsoni, Hotson's 5-toed jerboa
Many species of rodent have adapted to live in deserts, where few other mammals can survive. Here are three of them.

Fig. 3 Comparison of human kidney and desert rodent kidney

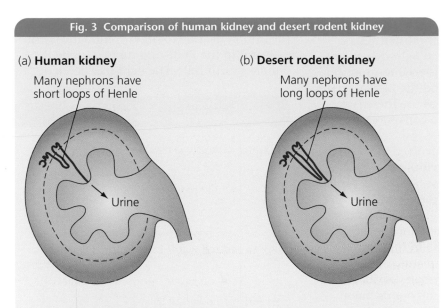

(a) **Human kidney**

Many nephrons have short loops of Henle

Urine

(b) **Desert rodent kidney**

Many nephrons have long loops of Henle

Urine

(c) **Nephron structure in a desert rodent**

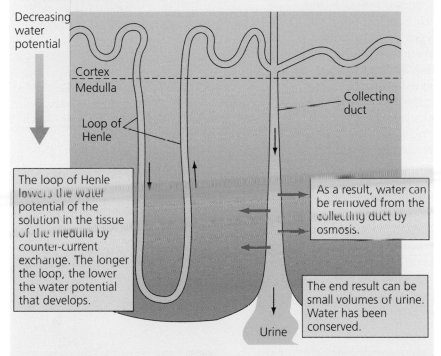

Decreasing water potential

Cortex
Medulla

Loop of Henle

Collecting duct

The loop of Henle lowers the water potential of the solution in the tissue of the medulla by counter-current exchange. The longer the loop, the lower the water potential that develops.

As a result, water can be removed from the collecting duct by osmosis.

The end result can be small volumes of urine. Water has been conserved.

Urine

In mammals that are not especially adapted for living in dry climates, only a relatively small proportion of the nephrons have long loops of Henle that dip down into the medulla of the kidneys. In humans, for example, only 14% of the loops are long ones, while in beavers none of them are. But in many desert rodents, practically all of the loops are long ones. What is more, these long loops are longer than those of non-desert living mammals. This means that the kidneys of desert rodents can build up a higher concentration of tissue fluid in the kidney medulla, and so produce a much more concentrated urine than other rodents. Tables 1 and 2 give some examples of the maximum concentration of urine that can be produced by different mammals.

Table 1 The maximum concentration of urine produced by some different mammals	
Mammal	**Approximate maximum urine concentration/ mosm dm^{-3}**
Desert mouse *Psammomys*	6000
Desert rat *Dipodomys*	6000
Red viscacha rat *Tympanochtomys*	7080
Camel	3000
Hamster	3000
Laboratory rat	3000
Human	1480
Pig	1100
Beaver	770

NB: mosm dm^{-3} (milliosmoles per cubic decimetre) is a measure of the concentration of the urine. The higher the number, the more concentrated the urine.

Table 2 Relative medullary thickness and maximum urine concentration in four desert rodents		
Rodent	**Relative medullary thickness**	**Maximum urine concentration/mosm dm^{-3}**
Calomys musculinus	12.3	8773
Eligmodontia typus	11.42	8612
Tympanochtomys barrerae	9.41	7080
Octomys mimax	6.09	2071

NB: The relative medullary thickness is a measure of how deep the medulla is compared with the overall size of the kidney. The larger the relative medullary thickness, the longer are the loops of Henle that dip into the medulla.

3a Summarise the relationship between habitat and maximum urine concentration, as shown in Table 1.

b With reference to the data in Table 2, suggest what pattern you would expect to find if you examined the lengths of the loops of Henle in the organisms listed in Table 1.

C$_4$ photosynthesis in tropical plants

You will remember that photosynthesis consists of two stages – the light-dependent reactions in which light is used to produce reduced NAD and ATP, and the light-independent reactions that use these two high-energy substances to convert carbon dioxide to carbohydrates.

One of the enzymes involved in the light-independent reactions is **ribulose bisphosphate carboxylase**, known as **rubisco**. Rubisco is thought to be the commonest enzyme in the world. It catalyses a reaction in which carbon dioxide is combined with a 5-carbon sugar called RuBP in the stroma of the chloroplasts. In most plants, this is the first reaction involving carbon dioxide and it produces two 3-carbon compounds; these plants are known as **C$_3$ plants**.

Unfortunately, rubisco can also catalyse the combination of *oxygen* with RuBP. Its tendency to do this increases as oxygen concentration, light intensity or temperature increase. So in many plants, as temperature and light intensity increase, **photosynthetic efficiency** decreases. More and more RuBP is wasted in a useless reaction involving oxygen, rather than being involved in producing carbohydrates.

Some plants have evolved a way around this problem. The RuBP and rubisco are kept inside **bundle sheath cells** (Fig. 4), well away from any of the air spaces in the leaf. However, this keeps the RuBP away from carbon dioxide as well as from oxygen. In these plants, an enzyme called **PEP carboxylase** catalyses the combination of carbon dioxide with a

compound called PEP. The PEP then passes on the carbon dioxide to other compounds, which deliver it to the RuBP and rubisco inside the bundle sheath cells. The light-independent

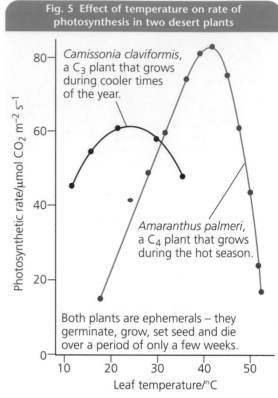

Fig. 5 Effect of temperature on rate of photosynthesis in two desert plants

Camissonia claviformis, a C$_3$ plant that grows during cooler times of the year.

Amaranthus palmeri, a C$_4$ plant that grows during the hot season.

Both plants are ephemerals – they germinate, grow, set seed and die over a period of only a few weeks.

Source: Fitter and Hay, *Environmental Physiology of Plants*, Academic Press, 1987

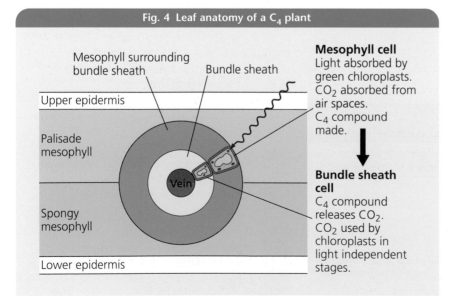

Fig. 4 Leaf anatomy of a C$_4$ plant

Mesophyll surrounding bundle sheath

Bundle sheath

Upper epidermis

Palisade mesophyll

Vein

Spongy mesophyll

Lower epidermis

Mesophyll cell
Light absorbed by green chloroplasts. CO$_2$ absorbed from air spaces. C$_4$ compound made.

Bundle sheath cell
C$_4$ compound releases CO$_2$. CO$_2$ used by chloroplasts in light independent stages.

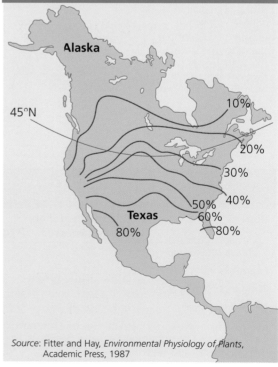

Fig. 6 Distribution of C$_4$ grasses in North America

Alaska

45°N

10%

20%

30%

40%

50%

60%

80%

Texas

80%

Source: Fitter and Hay, *Environmental Physiology of Plants*, Academic Press, 1987

reactions can then proceed as normal. In plants with this arrangement, the first carbon-containing compound that is made, when carbon dioxide combines with PEP, contains *four* carbon atoms. So these plants are known as **C$_4$ plants**. As you might expect, most C$_4$ plants grow in the tropics, where high light intensity and high temperature are most likely to occur. Many tropical grasses, for example, are C$_4$ plants.

PEP carboxylase is extremely efficient at picking up carbon dioxide, and so in C$_4$ plants the concentration of carbon dioxide in the air spaces inside the leaf is kept extremely low. This increases the diffusion gradient for carbon dioxide from the air

outside the leaf, so carbon dioxide moves in faster than it would in C$_3$ plants. As a result, C$_4$ plants tend to photosynthesise more rapidly than C$_3$ plants would do at the same carbon dioxide concentration, especially when temperature and light intensity are high (Fig. 5). Some of our most productive crop plants, such as maize, sorghum and sugar cane are C$_4$ plants. In cooler conditions there is less advantage in being a C$_4$ plant, and indeed C$_3$ plants may have higher productivities than C$_4$ plants in cool climates.

 4 Suggest an explanation for the distribution of C$_4$ grasses shown in Fig. 6.

3.3 Behavioural adaptation

A different way of coping with harsh environments is to avoid them by moving into habitats in which it is easier to live. Large and highly mobile animals, including many mammals and birds, can cover huge distances as they move from places where conditions are difficult into places where food, water or breeding sites are more abundant. Smaller animals, such as woodlice, are able to move away from difficult conditions into a microhabitat where they are able to survive more easily.

Bird migrations

The term 'migration' is normally used to describe diurnal (daily) or seasonal patterns of movement that relate to changing environmental conditions. Many species of bird have evolved behaviour patterns that

involve flying from one part of the world to another at different times of year. In Britain, average summer temperatures are significantly higher than those in winter. Birds, like mammals, are endothermic animals; they maintain a constant internal body temperature and can therefore remain active all the year round, so long as they can obtain enough food. Many birds remain in Britain throughout the year, and these are known as 'residents'. Some examples include robins and blackbirds.

Swallows are summer migrants. Swallows fly to Britain from Africa in the spring, often arriving in April as the days lengthen and temperatures rise. Their main food supply is flying insects, which they would not be able to find here during the winter months. They breed in Britain during the summer. The

Redwings eat berries, which are in ample supply in British hedgerows during the autumn and winter. Further north, in their breeding grounds, there would not be sufficient food for them in the winter months.

Fig. 7 Migration routes of redwings and swallows

(a) **Redwing**

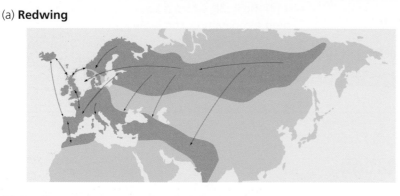

(b) **Swallow**

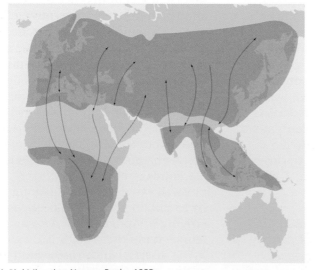

Source: Mead, *Bird Migration*, Newnes Books, 1983

young hatch in early summer when there is plenty of food available for them. In good years, the parents may also be able to rear a second brood before autumn brings cooler temperatures and shorter days. The parents then return to Africa and the young swallows often follow a few weeks later.

There are also several species of birds that are *winter* migrants to Britain. Redwings, for example, breed in northern Europe. They fly south to Britain in the autumn, often arriving in October.

Both swallows and redwings show similar migratory patterns (Fig. 7). They fly north in the summer, where they find suitable breeding grounds. They fly south in the winter, where they can find plenty of food that would not be available in their breeding places.

How do birds know when and where to migrate?

In many species of migratory bird, knowing *when* to migrate seems to be largely determined by changes in the bird's own body. The bird seems to have internally regulated annual changes in behaviour (such as increased restlessness) and in physiology (such as laying down extra fat that will be used as fuel during the long flight ahead). These changes do not depend on external factors such as changes in day-length. The factors that control the timing of migration are mostly **endogenous** ones. 'Endo' means 'within', so endogenous means that the control comes from *within* the bird's body.

It is likely that exogenous factors – factors in the bird's external environment – do at least help to fine-tune the timing of migratory behaviour. For example, if overcrowding begins to occur, or if food supplies start to run out early, then this may stimulate some species of birds to migrate slightly earlier than they normally would. They may also respond to changing day-length. The relative importance of exogenous and endogenous factors in the timing of migration almost certainly varies between different species of birds.

Knowing *where* to migrate – which route to take and where to stop – also seems to be controlled mostly by inbuilt mechanisms, which birds can use with a wide variety of navigational aids. They may, for example, use the Earth's magnetic field, the position of the Sun or the position of the stars to determine

CASE STUDY   **Evidence for endogenous control of migration**

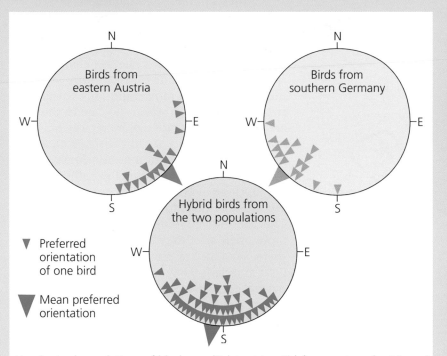

▼ Preferred
orientation
of one bird

▼ Mean preferred
orientation

Hand-raised populations of blackcaps (*Sylvia atricapilla*) from eastern Austria and southern Germany were kept in cages, and their orientation behaviour recorded at the time when they would normally migrate. The birds in the Austrian population showed a directional preference towards the SE while those in the German population preferred the SW. This matched the departure directions of birds in the wild in those areas. Hybrids between the two populations showed an intermediate choice of orientation direction.

Evidence for the endogenous control of the timing of migration has been obtained by observing the behaviour of captive birds. In one experiment, hand-raised garden warblers were kept in an environment where they had 10 hours of light and 14 hours of darkness, every day for 3 years. Even when there were no changing environmental factors to trigger migratory behaviour, the birds still showed increased restlessness and increased body mass around the time that they would migrate if they were living wild.

1 Suggest why hand-raised birds were used in this experiment.

It seems that inbuilt mechanisms also control the orientation birds take up at the start of migration. Evidence that this is so comes from the results of several experiments. One involving blackcaps is described opposite.

2 Using the evidence from the blackcap populations, suggest how young swallows know in which direction to fly to their winter feeding grounds, even if they are on their own.

their initial orientation, and then to keep them on course. The relative importance of these aids differs between species, and indeed some species may use other navigational aids that we know very little about. There are still many aspects of bird navigation that we do not understand, for example how birds sense magnetic fields.

As orientation at the start of migration is controlled genetically, it must have evolved over time. Birds that inherited alleles that sent them on suitable migration routes stayed alive and were able to breed, while those inheriting alleles that sent them in other directions were less likely to breed. Thus, the 'suitable direction' alleles become the most common ones in the population, while the 'unsuitable direction' alleles disappear. For land (as opposed to sea) birds, migration routes have often evolved to keep the travelling birds over land as much as possible, even if this means that the overall distance

travelled is longer than if they flew over the sea. Thus, many of the southward routes from Europe into Africa go over Spain and via the narrow straits of Gibraltar, rather than across the middle of the Mediterranean Sea. If weather conditions become poor, or if the bird's food reserves begin to run out, then the birds are never far from land, and can rest and feed before moving on.

Taxes and kineses

When we wish to move from place to place, we make a decision about where we want to go, and when and how we will move. For many invertebrates, however, the process is much simpler. They respond in an entirely predictable way to a particular stimulus. The same stimulus is likely always to produce the same response.

These simple responses to stimuli have evolved to increase the chances that an invertebrate will move away from harsh

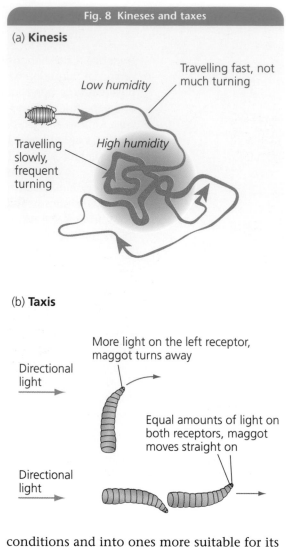

Fig. 8 Kineses and taxes

(a) **Kinesis**

Low humidity

Travelling fast, not much turning

Travelling slowly, frequent turning

High humidity

(b) **Taxis**

Directional light →

More light on the left receptor, maggot turns away

Equal amounts of light on both receptors, maggot moves straight on

Directional light →

responses that invertebrates show fall into two main categories – kineses and taxes.

A **kinesis** is a behavioural response to a stimulus in which the rate of movement, or the rate of turning, is affected by the external conditions. For example, if woodlice are placed in the centre of a choice chamber (Fig. 8) where one side is dry and the other is moist, they at first move randomly within the two areas. However, when they are in the dry area, they tend to move more rapidly and turn less than when they are in the moist area. After a while, this pattern of movement is likely to result in a huddle of woodlice within the moist area. The woodlice did not purposefully head towards the moist area. They just moved more slowly and turned more often once they happened to arrive there. Woodlice respond in a similar way to light and dark. The net result is that, in a natural ecosystem, woodlice are likely to congregate in the conditions where they are most likely to survive, such as beneath a rotting log. Here the humid atmosphere reduces water loss from their bodies, as well as keeping them relatively safe from predators.

A **taxis** does involve directional movement towards or away from a particular set of external conditions. If you place a blowfly maggot on a surface and shine a light onto it, it will move directly away from the light. Blowfly maggots feed on decaying flesh. In their natural environment, they would be found in and beneath rotting corpses. If one finds itself on the top of the dead body, in full light, its immediate response is to move away from the light and bury itself inside the corpse. Here, it has little problem of water loss, and is hidden from predators.

conditions and into ones more suitable for its survival. For example, invertebrates that do not have good structural or physiological mechanisms for conserving water tend to move into areas where the humidity is relatively high. The types of behavioural

1 The willow warbler is a small insect-eating bird. The shaded areas on the map show where willow warblers are found.

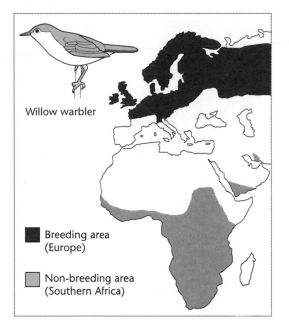

Willow warbler

■ Breeding area (Europe)

■ Non-breeding area (Southern Africa)

a What is the name given to the movement of animals such as the willow warbler from one area to another with changing seasons? (1)

b i) Suggest and explain at what time of year you would expect to find willow warblers in Europe.

   ii) Suggest why it is advantageous to willow warblers to move to Southern Africa for part of the year. (3)

NEAB BY05 February 1997 Q3

2 Polar bears are found in the extremely cold climate of the Arctic. Rabbits are found in warmer climates. Despite the differences in the temperatures they are exposed to, these animals both have fur with similar insulating properties.

a Suggest **two** ways, visible in the drawings, in which the polar bear is better adapted to low temperature than the rabbit. In each case explain your answer. (4)

b It is probable that the polar bear's ancestors were brown, as are other species of bear. Suggest how polar bears may have evolved from brown ancestors. (3)

NEAB BY05 February 1997 Q6

3 Heathland soil can be very dry during the summer. The diagrams show some of the xerophytic adaptations of bell heather, a typical heathland plant.

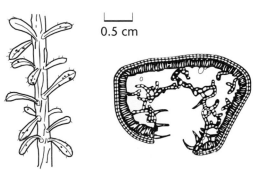

0.5 cm

Stem and leaves of bell heather

Section through a leaf of bell heather

a Describe and explain how **two** features of bell heather, visible in the diagrams, help to reduce water loss. (4)

Gorse is adapted to growing on heathland, where the soil is poor in nutrients. Gorse is a leguminous plant which forms a mutualistic relationship with nitrogen-fixing bacteria.

b Describe how each organism benefits from this relationship. (4)

NEAB BY05 March 1998

4 Agricultural ecosystems

Nowadays, almost all of our food – apart from much of the seafood we consume – comes from agriculture.

Early humans were hunter–gatherers. They collected food – both plant and animal – from naturally occurring sources around them. In Britain, the major sources of food were fruits, nuts and seeds, and also a variety of wild animals. Mammals such as deer and wild boar were hunted and killed. Animal food also came from the sea, and fish and shellfish formed an important part of the diet of these early people. We still act as hunter–gatherers today, when we harvest fish and shellfish from the sea. This is discussed in Chapter 5.

About 10 000 years ago, people in Britain began to take much more control over the sources of their food. They changed from being hunter–gatherers to agriculturalists. They had already domesticated dogs, which must have helped with hunting wild animals. Now they began to domesticate wild animals too, including cattle, sheep, goats and pigs. Crops were planted, tended and harvested, to provide food and other resources, such as clothing and building materials.

In this chapter, we will consider how agricultural ecosystems compare with natural ones. We will also look at how we can maximise yields from the crops we grow, by controlling abiotic and biotic factors that may limit plant growth.

4.1   Agricultural and natural ecosystems compared

In Chapter 1, we saw how communities can gradually change over time, a process known as succession. When farmers use land to grow crops, they are effectively stopping succession from occurring. Left to its own devices, a wheat field would eventually become woodland. Modern farming usually involves clearing the land once a year, before planting with the crop. No plant is allowed to get a permanent foothold, apart from the crop plants.

Species diversity and genetic diversity

If a wheat field were allowed to follow its natural succession, its species diversity would increase greatly.

In a wheat field – especially if weeds are controlled – there is essentially only a single species of plant. This is known as a **monoculture**. There may be some animals – insects, for example, that feed on the wheat plants – but there will not be many different kinds of these because there is such a small variety of habitats and food sources. If the farmer regularly sprays with insecticides, then the species diversity will be very low indeed Usually, the species diversity on agricultural land is much lower than the species diversity of a natural ecosystem.

It is highly likely that the **genetic diversity** within the wheat crop is also extremely low. Thousands of years ago, as people harvested their crop of wheat grains, they would have put aside some of these grains to sow next year. They would have chosen to save grain from the plants with the best characteristics – for example, high yield, resistance to damage by insects or fungi, a tendency to hold on to the grain rather than shed it onto the ground before harvest. So, even if the field contained wheat plants with a wide variety of different alleles, the selected seeds would only contain a proportion of these. Each time such selection took place, more alleles would be lost. Today, with more sophisticated breeding techniques, each wheat variety is essentially homozygous for every single gene. Every wheat plant in the whole field is genetically identical to every other wheat plant in that field.

This homozygosity is advantageous to the farmer. So long as soil and climate conditions are the same throughout the field, then every plant will grow to the same height and ripen at the same time, making mechanical harvesting very easy. The grain that is harvested will be of uniform quality, making it more valuable to processors such as flour producers, and therefore of high marketing value to the farmer.

There are, however, some disadvantages to homozygosity. Although that particular wheat variety will have been bred to grow well and give high yields in certain conditions, it will be very vulnerable to change. For example, if a new fungus pest appears to which the variety is susceptible, then every plant will succumb. Or, if a farmer attempts to grow this variety in a different climate, it may not be successful. For this reason, **gene banks** have been set up for many important crop plants, to conserve as much genetic diversity as possible. In most cases, the gene banks consist of stores of seeds, which can be germinated to produce plants that could be used in future breeding programmes.

Productivity – the quantitative basis of crop production

When crop plants are grown for food, we are essentially using the plants to convert energy in sunlight into chemical energy in carbohydrates and other nutrients. The rate at which plants do this is known as **primary productivity**.

Primary productivity is often measured in terms of the amount of energy that is converted from light energy into chemical energy, over an area of one square metre, during one year. Its units are, therefore, $kJ\ m^{-2}\ year^{-1}$. Another way of measuring it is the mass of new plant matter that is produced, over an area of one square metre, per day. In this case, its units are $g\ m^{-2}\ day^{-1}$. Table 1 shows productivity per day in $g\ m^{-2}$.

Table 1 Crop productivity		
Crop	**Productivity per day of growing season/g m^{-2}**	
	World average	**Highest yield**
Wheat	2.3	8.3
Oats	2.4	6.2
Maize	2.3	4.4
Rice	2.7	4.4
Potatoes	2.6	5.6
Sugar beet	4.3	8.2

Source: WWF

The rate at which photosynthetic products accumulate is the gross primary productivity (GPP). However, plants use up some of the dry mass and release energy from it during respiration. The net gain of dry mass stored in the plant after respiration is known as the net primary productivity (NPP). This represents potential food available to primary consumers – that is, herbivores.

$$\text{Net productivity} = \text{gross productivity} - \text{respiratory loss}$$

Table 2 gives some values for NPP in a range of different ecosystems. You can see that intensive agriculture (where the land is farmed to get as a high a yield as possible, by using inputs such as pesticides and inorganic fertilisers) comes very high in the list, second only to tropical rainforests.

Table 2 NPP values	
Ecosystem	NPP/kJ m^{-2} $year^{-1}$
Extreme desert	260
Desert scrub	2 600
Subsistence agriculture	3 000
Open ocean	4 700
Areas over continental shelf	13 500
Temperate grasslands	15 000
Temperate deciduous forest	26 000
Intensive agriculture	30 000
Tropical forest	40 000

Source: The Open University, Foundation Science Course

Primary productivity is affected by a wide range of abiotic and biotic factors. Productivity is directly related to the rate of photosynthesis. The rate at which plants can photosynthesise is determined by:

- the intrinsic capabilities of the particular species and variety of plants;
- the intensity of sunlight that falls onto them;
- the duration of light each day;
- the amount of water that is available;
- the temperature;
- the concentration of carbon dioxide in the atmosphere;
- the availability of inorganic ions such as nitrate in the soil;
- competition for light and other resources;
- damage to the plants by fungi, insects and other pests.

1a Which of the factors listed above are abiotic factors, and which are biotic factors?

b Suggest which factors are likely to contribute to the high productivity in the two most productive ecosystems in Table 2.

c Suggest which factors are likely to be reducing productivity in the two least productive ecosystems in Table 2.

4.2 Increasing productivity

As well as being influenced by a range of abiotic and biotic factors, productivity is affected by the number of leaves a plant has and the efficiency with which it can convert the sunlight energy falling on those leaves into chemical energy.

Photosynthetic efficiency

Productivity depends on the intrinsic photosynthetic abilities of particular species and varieties of crop plants. Different crop plants vary in the efficiency with which they are able to convert sunlight energy into chemical energy. Photosynthetic efficiency is a measure of how successful a plant is at using the sunlight that falls onto its leaves, to make carbohydrates and other substances by photosynthesis.

$$\text{Photosynthetic efficiency} = \frac{\text{amount of energy stored in newly formed carbohydrates}}{\text{amount of light energy that falls on the plant}}$$

About 45% of sunlight falling on a plant is within the photosynthetically active radiation (PAR) waveband. Up to 85% of PAR is actually absorbed (see Fig. 1).

So the efficiency of light absorption is:

$$\frac{45 \times 85}{100} = 38.25\%$$

Chloroplasts operate at about 20% efficiency so the *maximum* overall efficiency of photosynthesis is:

$$\frac{38.25 \times 20}{100} = 7.65\% \text{ (i.e. about 8\%)}$$

Photosynthetic efficiency is usually a lot lower than 8% because of factors such as low temperature, plant dormancy and the plant's own energy needs for respiration (Table 3, overleaf).

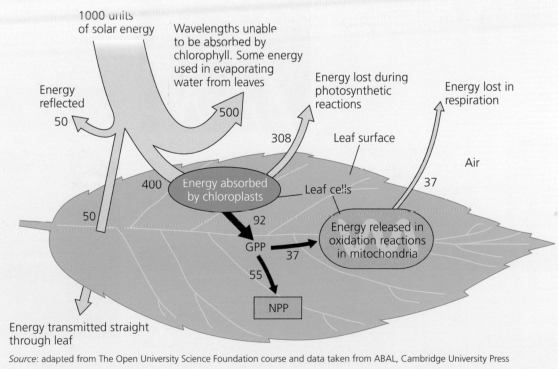

Fig. 1 Photosynthetic efficiency

The amount of solar energy intercepted by green plants depends a great deal on geographical location. In Britain, this is estimated as approximately 1×10^6 kJ m^{-2} year^{-1}, but at least 95% of this is unavailable to plants for photosynthesis.

Source: adapted from The Open University Science Foundation course and data taken from ABAL, Cambridge University Press

Table 3 Photosynthetic efficiency		
	Sugar beet (temperate crop)	Sugar cane (tropical crop)
Mean solar energy during growing season (MJ m^{-2} day^{-1})	10.9	20.9
Carbohydrate production at 8% efficiency (maximum theoretical) (g m^{-2} day^{-1})	60 (8%)	104 (8%)
Maximum recorded experimentally over a short period (g m^{-2} day^{-1})	31 (4%)	43 (3%)
Seasonal mean for commercial farming (g m^{-2} day^{-1})	9 (1.2%)	10 (0.8%)

Source: The Open University

Sugar beet

Sugar cane

2 Using Table 4, calculate the value for NPP of maize.

Table 4 Energy budget		
	Glucose/kg	% of solar energy
Solar energy		100
Respiration of maize	2045	0.4
GPP of maize	8732	1.6

Measurements are of half a hectare of maize during a growing season of 100 days.

Source: The Open University

Leaf area index

If the crop plant has leaves that cover all of the field, then every kilojoule of sunlight will fall onto them. If, however, the leaves only cover part of that area, then much of the sunlight will fall onto bare soil. The percentage of the ground that is covered by the crop plant's leaves is known as the **leaf area index (LAI)**.

$$LAI = \frac{LA \text{ (leaf area)}}{GA \text{ (ground area)}} \times 100$$

For example, if a crop has 3 m^2 of leaf area above 10 m^2 of ground, the LAI is 30%. LAI gives an indication of the amount of light the crop can intercept. Crops with a higher LAI will absorb more light, so potentially have a higher photosynthetic rate. As LAI increases, so does productivity. Obviously, the more leaf area there is to catch the sunlight, then the more photosynthesis will be taking place.

In temperate areas, the maximum LAI is between 20% and 100%. As LAI increases, there is more likelihood that lower leaves will be shaded by upper leaves. In tropical areas, the higher solar energy means that the LAI may be greater than 200%. This means that, on average, every lower leaf has another leaf above it. Obviously, the lower leaves will not be getting as much sunlight at those above them. Thus, a field in which LAI is 200% will not have twice the productivity of a field where LAI is 100%.

In a crop that has just germinated, the LAI will be low because the leaf area is insignificant compared to the ground area. As the crop grows the LAI increases.

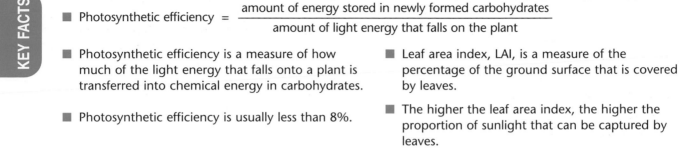

■ Photosynthetic efficiency = $\dfrac{\text{amount of energy stored in newly formed carbohydrates}}{\text{amount of light energy that falls on the plant}}$

■ Photosynthetic efficiency is a measure of how much of the light energy that falls onto a plant is transferred into chemical energy in carbohydrates.

■ Photosynthetic efficiency is usually less than 8%.

■ Leaf area index, LAI, is a measure of the percentage of the ground surface that is covered by leaves.

■ The higher the leaf area index, the higher the proportion of sunlight that can be captured by leaves.

Energy input – extensive and intensive farming

Farming practices differ enormously in different countries, and even in different regions of one country. In some countries, and in some areas of Britain, land is farmed using very few or no inputs of fertilisers or other chemicals. This is called **extensive farming**. Farmers spend relatively little money on the land. Sheep grazing on upland areas such as the Pennines are extensively farmed. No fertiliser is used on the land, so productivity of the grass is quite low, and not many sheep can be supported on one hectare.

In contrast, much of Britain is farmed intensively. **Intensive farming** is geared to getting the maximum crop, or the maximum amount of milk or meat, from an area of land. In order to achieve high outputs, high inputs of fertilisers and pesticides are needed. There is also high energy input in terms of the fossil fuels used to drive farm machinery and in the manufacture of fertilisers and pesticides. Farmers spend much more money than they would if they farmed extensively, but this is offset by the higher income received from the larger crop.

Free-range hens like these are extensively farmed.

Chickens kept in battery houses are intensively farmed.

Farming in Britain since the mid 20th century

In the early years of the 20th century in Britain, farming was mostly extensive. Most farms were mixed farms – some land was used for growing crops, and some for raising animals for milk, wool or meat. Animal dung was used to fertilise the arable land. Winter feed for the animals was produced from the crops. Work on the land was labour-intensive, and use of fertilisers and other chemicals was low.

After two world wars in the first half of the 20th century, it became very difficult to import enough food. Farmers in Britain were encouraged to produce as much food as they could from their land. Rapid changes in farming practice began, and continued during the latter half of the 20th century, as farming moved rapidly from extensive to intensive. Inputs of fertilisers soared. Motorised machinery replaced horses. Crop yields per hectare of land rocketed.

Similar trends have occurred throughout western Europe and indeed in all other developed countries. However, people have begun to question the environmental wisdom of farming in this intensive way.

Do we need to produce quite so much from our land? Are the high energy inputs, in terms of fossil fuels used in machinery and in the manufacture of fertilisers, justifiable in a world threatened by global warming and in which non-renewable fuel sources are fast running out? Are we happy with the effects that pesticides have on species diversity? In Britain today, many farmers are converting to **organic farming**. This involves growing crops or rearing animals without the use of artificial fertilisers, pesticides or herbicides.

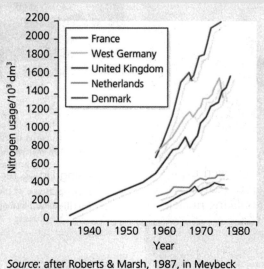

Source: after Roberts & Marsh, 1987, in Meybeck *et al.*, 1989, adapted from AHS publication 164

Nitrogen fertiliser in Western Europe.

1 Outline the possible environmental effects of the increase in fertiliser use shown in the graph.

Crop rotation and fertilisers

If you look back to Table 1 on page 47, you will see that the average productivity for each crop is much less than the highest yields recorded. The productivity of a crop may be prevented from reaching its potential maximum by many different factors, both abiotic and biotic. Among the abiotic factors is the availability of mineral ions.

Mineral ions from fertilisers

Plants require many different inorganic ions (sometimes called minerals) that they obtain from the soil, taking them into their root hairs by diffusion or active transport. Of these ions, the ones that are most likely to be in short supply are nitrates, phosphates and potassium.

Nitrates are needed for the manufacture of amino acids, and therefore proteins, in the plant. Although air contains almost 80% nitrogen, this gas (N_2) is far too unreactive to be useful to a plant. Plants can only use nitrogen from a more reactive compound, such as nitrate (NO_3^-) or ammonium (NH_4^+) ions. Supplying plants with nitrogen means supplying nitrates or ammonium salts.

Phosphorus is needed for making nucleic acids – DNA and RNA – and also ATP. It is important in many enzyme-catalysed reactions in plants. It is also vital for cell division and is needed in areas of rapid early growth. If phosphorus is lacking, root growth is stunted. Nitrogen and phosphorus interact to affect crop growth. Plants absorb phosphorus in the form of phosphate ions (PO_4^{2-}).

Potassium is important in maintaining the balance of negative and positive ions inside and outside cells, and is involved in protein metabolism. Efficient photosynthesis and active transport rely on an adequate supply of potassium. If it is not available, leaves turn yellow and smaller grain forms.

To achieve good yields, farmers apply fertilisers containing these ions to the soil. They may use an **artificial fertiliser** or a **natural fertiliser**. Inorganic or artificial fertilisers consist of inorganic compounds like ammonium nitrate. Organic or natural fertilisers consist of organic materials such as animal manures, composts and sewage sludge.

Good farming practice involves measuring the concentration of inorganic ions in the soil, and calculating the amount that will be required by whatever crop is to be grown.

This enables exactly the right amount of the right type of fertiliser to be applied. Different crops require a different balance of minerals. The NPK value of a crop is the ratio of nitrogen:phosphorus:potassium needed. Spring barley usually has a NPK value of 2:1:1, whereas legumes (peas, beans, clover and alfalfa), which do not need to obtain nitrogen from the soil, have a value of 0:1:1.

When an ion such as nitrate is in short supply, adding some of it to the soil will increase growth. Up to a point, the more you add the better the growth that results. However, after a certain level, the beneficial effect on growth begins to tail off. Applying too much fertiliser can actually *reduce* the growth of the crop (Fig. 2). This is called the **law of diminishing returns**. Economically, because of the high cost of fertiliser, it may be better not to apply quite as much as would be required to achieve the very highest possible yield.

> **3** Using Fig. 2, recommend the most appropriate concentration of nitrogen fertiliser for this crop. Give your reasons.

The availabilities of different ions interact in terms of their effects on crop growth. For example, if a sugar beet plant is short of phosphorus, then it may not be able to make maximum use of the nitrate that is available to it.

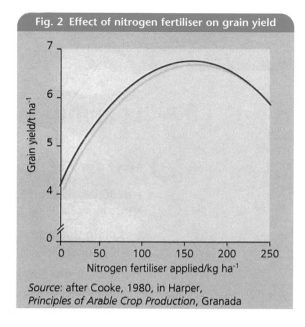

Fig. 2 Effect of nitrogen fertiliser on grain yield

Source: after Cooke, 1980, in Harper, *Principles of Arable Crop Production*, Granada

4 Suggest the limiting factor on root yield for each curve in Fig. 3.

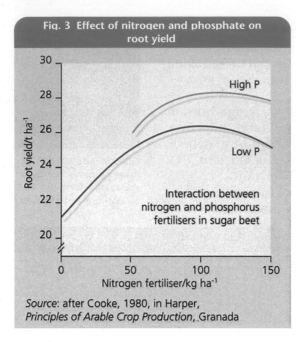

Fig. 3 Effect of nitrogen and phosphate on root yield

High P

Low P

Interaction between nitrogen and phosphorus fertilisers in sugar beet

Source: after Cooke, 1980, in Harper, *Principles of Arable Crop Production*, Granada

Choosing and applying fertilisers

Inorganic fertilisers have a high nutrient content. The amounts and ratios of plant nutrients are known, and can be matched to the needs of the crop. In contrast, the nutrient content of organic fertiliser varies depending on the animal species and its diet, and it can be very difficult to match the nutrient needs of the crop exactly.

If soil is very low in nitrogen and a nitrogen-demanding crop is to be grown, then the speed of release of nutrients from the fertiliser used may influence a farmer's choice. Ammonium nitrate, used in inorganic fertilisers, is very soluble and releases nitrates to the soil easily. Urea, found in organic fertiliser, gives a much slower rate of release. However, some nutrients in organic fertilisers are present in a soluble, readily available form, and more nutrients are released over a longer time by the decomposition of organic matter by microorganisms. One application of organic fertiliser can have a much longer-lasting effect than inorganic fertiliser (Table 5).

Fertilisers need to be added to the soil ready for when the crop's demand for nutrients is at its greatest. Nitrates and ammonium ions are highly soluble and during periods of rainfall there is a risk of

Organic fertiliser can be bulky and difficult to handle and apply to the soil.

Table 5 Crop yields using different fertilisers				
Crop	Control (no fertiliser)	FYM only	NPK only	FYM as % of NPK
Wheat	2.08	3.50	3.11	112
Barley	1.03	2.03	2.26	90
Sugar beet	3.80	15.60	15.60	100
Mangolds (beet for cattle)	3.80	22.30	30.90	72

The yield of crops as t ha^{-1} is given after long-term applications of farmyard manures (FYM) and inorganic fertilisers (NPK).

Source: Haywood, *Applied Ecology*, Nelson, 1992

nutrient loss due to leaching (drainage of nutrients dissolved in water through the soil). Nitrogen is rarely applied during autumn because of the danger of leaching during the wet winter months. For autumn-sown crops, nitrogen is added in two stages. An early application, in late February to early March stimulates the growth of side shoots. A second application in late April to early May replaces nutrient loss by leaching due to spring rains. With spring-sown crops such as spring barley, potatoes and sugar beet, the nitrogen is applied either just before sowing or at the same time as the seed.

Potassium and phosphates are not very soluble, so losses from the soil by leaching are small. These nutrients are usually ploughed into the soil just before sowing.

Inorganic fertilisers are expensive and farmers do not want to use more than they must. The value of the increased yield is known as the yield return. This must be greater than the cost of applying the fertiliser. The value of the increased yield minus the cost of the fertiliser application is called the maximum net yield.

The cost–benefit ratio is the value of the yield return divided by the cost of applying the fertiliser chosen. Eventually there is a point at which the application of extra nitrogen fertiliser is not covered by the value of the increased yield. This is an example of the law of diminishing returns. There is less return from the crop from increased fertiliser applications.

5a Draw a graph of the data in Table 6.

b Describe any relationship that you can observe.

c The value of the crop in Table 6 is £100 per tonne and the fertiliser costs 50p per kg. Calculate the cost–benefit ratio for each fertiliser application.

d Does the yield return exceed the cost for all fertiliser applications?

e Which fertiliser application would you think is most economical? Explain your answer.

Farmers also have to consider the costs of machinery and labour. Many inorganic fertilisers come in granules or pellets and specialised machinery is needed for spreading them over the land. However, the machinery is light, and the fertiliser is easy to store and to handle. If kept in moisture-proof conditions, the fertiliser can be stored for long periods of time.

Organic fertilisers like farmyard manure (FYM) are bulky and difficult to store. There may be insufficient organic material available on site and it may have to be transported from livestock areas into arable (used for crop production) areas. Heavy machinery is needed to handle the fertiliser, and it can be difficult to apply evenly over a field. Weed seeds and fungal spores that cause plant diseases may be present in animal manures. Sewage sludge may contain heavy metals such as lead, zinc and nickel, which can be toxic to plants. On the other hand, organic matter binds the soil particles together. This improves the overall soil structure by aiding aeration and drainage in clay soils, and water retention in light, sandy soils. Organic material also acts as a food resource for soil organisms, and the activity of animals such as earthworms also improves soil aeration and drainage. Organic matter releases nutrients over a longer period of time as a result of the action of microorganisms.

Recycling organic waste makes good environmental sense. The nutrients in the organic material are added to soil where they will be used up by crops. If organic material is just left, for example in land fill sites, then there can be problems of uncontrolled leaching.

Mineral ions and crop rotation

Each crop takes a particular balance of mineral ions from the soil. If you grow the same crop year after year after year on the same land, then the soil becomes depleted of those ions.

In the past, most farmers grew different crops in successive years. This is called **crop rotation**. Many rotations include **legumes**, such as peas, beans or clover. The legumes increase the amount of nitrate or ammonium ions in the soil, because their roots have nodules containing nitrogen-fixing bacteria. Usually, at harvest, the roots of the legumes are left in the soil and are ploughed in before the next crop is planted. An example of crop

Table 6 Yield return of a cereal crop					
N applied/kg ha^{-1}	0	50	100	150	200
Yield/t ha^{-1}	2.9	3.4	4.3	4.7	4.8

Source: Harper, *Principles of Arable Crop Production*, Granada

rotation that was widely used towards the end of the 19th century is shown in Fig. 4 (a ley is a grass and legume mix that can be grazed by livestock; the animals' faeces help to add mineral ions and humus to the soil). However, the easy availability of inorganic fertilisers has led to crop specialisation and the loss of traditional crop rotations.

Moreover, reliance on inorganic fertilisers can result in lower organic matter in the soil, which then supports fewer soil organisms and has a poorer soil structure. In organic farming, crop rotation comes into its own again. Instead of soluble inorganic fertilisers, the organic farmer relies on crop rotation together with organic manures and composts, crop residues and off-farm organic wastes like spent mushroom compost.

Crop rotation influences the amounts of nutrients that need to be added for different crops. Winter wheat grown after another cereal needs far more of each nutrient than it does if grown after root crops. This is because a root crop takes up far less nutrients than a cereal crop.

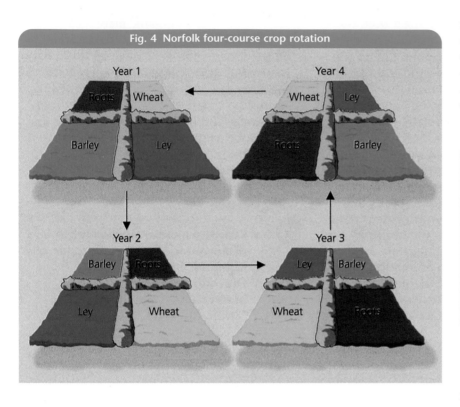

Fig. 4 Norfolk four-course crop rotation

6a From Table 7, compare the difference in recommended levels of fertiliser application for spring barley grown after cereals and grown after roots.

b How do the nutrient demands of winter wheat (grown after cereals) compare with those of sugar beet?

c What might happen if these recommended levels of fertilisers were: exceeded; not met?

As well as reducing the quantity of fertiliser that needs to be applied, crop rotation has other benefits. Different crops need different methods of cultivation, which leads to improved soil texture. Growing different crops breaks the life-cycles of crop pests and disease-causing organisms. There is less chance of pests and diseases associated with a particular crop becoming established. Keeping the soil covered by growing crops all the year round helps to prevent erosion and leaching. Growing an early crop, like winter wheat, in the rotation, means that it is more difficult for certain weeds to germinate and become established. Growing a crop in the rotation that will be grazed by livestock over the winter means that nutrients in the soil are used over the winter. As a result there is less likelihood of nutrient loss by leaching, and organic matter is returned to the soil in the animals' faeces. For all of these reasons, even intensive farming now frequently uses some form of crop rotation.

Crop	Fertiliser recommendations/kg ha^{-1}		
	N	P	K
Winter wheat after cereals	150–200	50–100	50–100
Winter wheat after roots	50–100	40–60	0–60
Spring barley after cereals	125–150	50–100	50–100
Spring barley after roots	40–75	40–60	0–60
Sugar beet	125–150	65–125	150–200
Potatoes	120–200	150–220	150–250
Oilseed rape	120–200	60–80	60–80
Maize	100–150	60–90	60–90
Mown grass	200–400	80–100	60–200
Grazed grass	150–350	50–60	60–100

Table 7 Fertiliser recommendations

Source: Haywood, *Applied Ecology*, Nelson, 1992

- Plants need a variety of inorganic ions, which they obtain from the soil.

- The ions that are most commonly in short supply in soil are nitrates, phosphates and potassium.

- Fertilisers replace the nutrients that the harvested crop has removed.

- The correct amount of NPK fertiliser will allow crops to achieve their full growth potential if no other factor is limiting.

- Inorganic fertilisers are expensive, but they are easy to apply and store and are rich in easily released nutrients.

- Organic fertilisers are difficult to store and apply but have a long-lasting effect and are cheaper.

- A farmer has to consider the economics of applying fertiliser to maintain high, sustainable yields.

- After a certain level of application, adding more fertiliser has only a small positive effect on crop yields, and at very high levels of application may even reduce yields. This is known as the law of diminishing returns.

- Crop rotation can reduce the amount of fertiliser that is needed each year.

- Legumes are valuable in a crop rotation because the nitrogen-fixing bacteria in their root nodules add nitrogen-containing compounds to the soil.

4.3 Abiotic factors and photosynthesis

Productivity is also affected by a number of abiotic factors that directly affect photosynthesis: temperature, carbon dioxide concentration, light intensity and water availability.

Speeding up photosynthesis

The rate of photosynthesis is important in food production because it determines the crop yield. Many factors can affect the rate of photosynthesis of a crop. Environmental factors include light, temperature, carbon dioxide, water and nutrients. Good crop management involves the manipulation of these factors in order to maximise photosynthesis and achieve good yields.

If one of these environmental factors falls below a certain level, it will start to limit the rate of photosynthesis. Although temperature, carbon dioxide and light may all affect photosynthesis, only the one that is in the shortest supply will limit the rate at any particular moment. This factor is called the **limiting factor**. The rate of photosynthesis can be increased by increasing that factor.

Light

The effect of light on photosynthesis depends on:

- light quality – that is, the wavelengths that it contains; plants can make use of only certain wavelengths for photosynthesis;

- light duration – that is, the day length;

- light intensity – that is, how strong the light is.

Day length may be limited to 8 hours in winter in Britain, but can be double that in summer. The period of the year when day length is greatest coincides with the period when the light intensity is highest. In Britain, this is midday in June. The total amount of solar energy available to a crop equals light intensity × time. In tropical countries, the amount of solar energy available can be fairly constant throughout the year.

At low light intensities, an increase in the rate of photosynthesis is directly proportional to increasing light intensity (Fig. 5). But

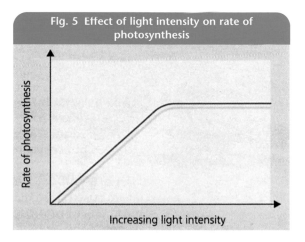

Fig. 5 Effect of light intensity on rate of photosynthesis

Rate of photosynthesis

Increasing light intensity

eventually, the process reaches a maximum rate and fails to increase further. This could be because:

- the photosynthetic reactions are proceeding as fast as is possible for the photosynthetic 'machinery' in that particular plant;
- some other factor is now limiting the rate, such as carbon dioxide concentration or temperature.

The maximum amount of light that can be used in photosynthetic reactions is estimated to be about 10 000 lux. On a clear summer's day, solar illumination may reach 100 000 lux. At this time of year, therefore, light intensity is not the limiting factor. However, at very high light intensities there may be damage to the chlorophyll molecules, resulting in a drop in the rate of photosynthesis.

Temperature
When light intensity is high, increasing temperature can have an effect on the rate of photosynthesis. Between the range 10 °C to about 35 °C, a 10 °C rise in the temperature will double the rate of photosynthesis (Fig. 6).

7a In Fig. 6, what is the limiting factor of curve A?

b Suggest why the rate of photosynthesis drops at the point marked **X**.

Carbon dioxide
In tropical areas, temperature and light intensity are not usually the limiting factors of photosynthesis; carbon dioxide is. Carbon dioxide is the source of carbon atoms used to make all the organic products of photosynthesis. Carbon dioxide is needed in the light-independent reactions of photosynthesis, where it is reduced to carbohydrate and other organic compounds. Atmospheric carbon dioxide is usually about 0.03% of the volume of the air. For most plants, this is lower than the optimum value for photosynthesis. So, under normal conditions for crops, carbon dioxide is often the limiting factor (Figs. 7 and 8).

 Using Fig. 8, which curve shows carbon dioxide concentration to have the greatest effect as a limiting factor?

Water
In arid areas, water is the overriding factor affecting crop yield. Periods of temporary wilting can lead to heavy losses in crop yield.

The rate of photosynthesis falls when plants are water-stressed. This is unlikely to be because there is not enough water for the light-dependent stage of photosynthesis. It is

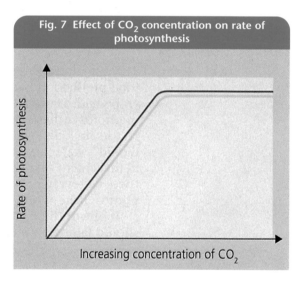

Fig. 7 Effect of CO_2 concentration on rate of photosynthesis

Rate of photosynthesis

Increasing concentration of CO_2

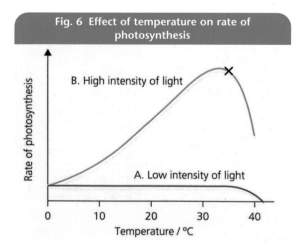

Fig. 6 Effect of temperature on rate of photosynthesis

Rate of photosynthesis

B. High intensity of light

A. Low intensity of light

0   10   20   30   40
Temperature / °C

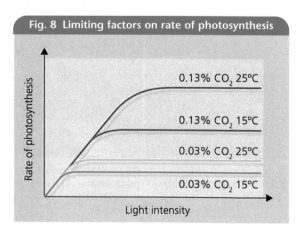

Fig. 8 Limiting factors on rate of photosynthesis

Rate of photosynthesis

0.13% CO_2 25°C

0.13% CO_2 15°C

0.03% CO_2 25°C

0.03% CO_2 15°C

Light intensity

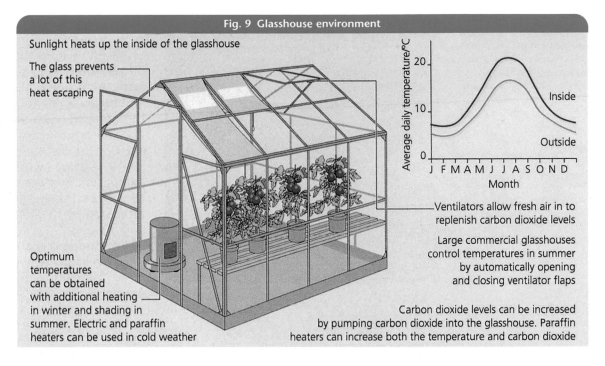

Fig. 9 Glasshouse environment

Sunlight heats up the inside of the glasshouse

The glass prevents a lot of this heat escaping

Optimum temperatures can be obtained with additional heating in winter and shading in summer. Electric and paraffin heaters can be used in cold weather

Ventilators allow fresh air in to replenish carbon dioxide levels

Large commercial glasshouses control temperatures in summer by automatically opening and closing ventilator flaps

Carbon dioxide levels can be increased by pumping carbon dioxide into the glasshouse. Paraffin heaters can increase both the temperature and carbon dioxide

far more likely to be because of more indirect effects caused by water shortage. One of the first consequences of lack of water is that the stomata close. This cuts off the carbon dioxide supply to photosynthesising cells. It is impossible to measure the direct effects of water shortage on photosynthesis because it is used in so many other cell processes.

Glasshouse management

In order to achieve maximum yields, possible limiting factors need to be controlled. If the physical environment can be modified, the growth of crops can be regulated. This may not be possible in the case of a crop grown outside. However, by growing crops under glass or plastic greater control of environmental conditions is possible (Fig. 9). Glasshouse cultivation allows:

- better yields to be achieved;
- some crops to be grown out of season and so provide a better economic return;
- some plants to be grown in regions where they would not normally grow.

Over short periods, 0.5% carbon dioxide has been found to be the optimum concentration for photosynthesis. Over longer periods, however, this concentration may cause the stomata to close, resulting in a drop in photosynthesis. For glasshouse crops like tomatoes, 0.1% carbon dioxide is the optimum over long periods.

Tomatoes can be sown at a minimum daily temperature of 10 °C and die off when the temperature falls below about 2 °C. Temperatures above 28 °C can damage tomato plants.

Artificial lighting can be used in glasshouses when the natural light intensity falls too low. Shading out strong light is achieved by large mechanically operated blinds. Many glasshouses have automatic watering systems with sprinklers and humidifiers. It is important to regulate humidity to control fungal diseases, which can increase when the humidity is too high.

All of these factors can be controlled by computers. Sensors are used to monitor the level of each factor and the feedback is processed by the computer.

4.4 Chemical control of weeds and insects

Besides the abiotic factors affecting crop yields, there are many biotic factors to take into consideration. These include:

- intraspecific competition – that is, competition between individual crop plants growing together for light, water and inorganic ions;

- interspecific competition – that is, competition between the crop plants and plants of other species growing in the field;

- grazing by herbivores such as rabbits or insects;

- parasitism and disease, for example fungi growing on the crop plants, or infection with disease-causing bacteria or viruses.

Farmers avoid too much intraspecific competition by planting crops at the optimum density. Too sparse sowing results in a low LAI and a relatively low yield; too dense sowing results in plants not reaching their full potential because of competition with other plants, so the extra seed that was planted is wasted.

Plants of other species growing among crop plants are known as **weeds**. They can be controlled by using chemicals called **herbicides**, or by non-chemical methods such as hoeing, or by using biological control.

Insects or fungi that feed on crop plants are **pests**, and the chemicals that are used to control them are **pesticides**. These include **insecticides** and **fungicides**. Non-chemical methods of control can be also used, including **biological control**.

World-wide crop losses caused by insects, weeds and diseases are shown in Fig. 10.

Chemical control of weeds

A weed is a plant growing in the wrong place at the wrong time, competing with the crop plant and so reducing crop yield. Weeds also cause a reduction in yields because they act as hosts for pests and disease-causing organisms. For example, fungi can survive in many grass species and then infect cereal crops. Seeds from weeds can get mixed up in harvested seed, and be sown along with the crop seed.

A wide range of herbicides is available for farmers to use in order to reduce competition from weeds in fields of crops. Some herbicides are **non-selective**, or **broad-spectrum**. This means they kill any plant, including crop plants. They can only be used before a crop has been sown or before germination. They can be used to clear areas before cultivation. Other herbicides are **selective**. They have been developed to affect only certain types of plant. For example, they may kill broad-leaved plants – which includes most weeds – but do not kill plants with narrow leaves such as wheat and other cereals. They can be applied after a crop has germinated.

An example of a selective herbicide is 2,4-D. This is a synthetic auxin. Auxins are chemicals that are produced in the growing regions of plants, in very small quantities. Auxins affect the growth and development of plants. They are plant hormones, sometimes known as plant growth regulators. The auxin 2,4-D has a very similar molecular structure to the most common naturally produced auxin, known as IAA. When 2,4-D is sprayed onto a field of wheat, it makes the broad-leaved weeds grow very quickly for a short while, and then die. The wheat is not affected.

Herbicides may also be classified as **contact herbicides** and **systemic herbicides**.

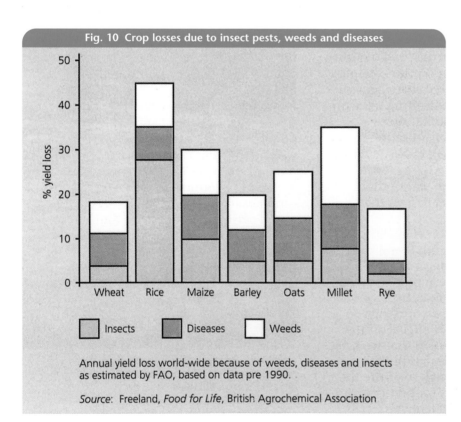

Fig. 10 Crop losses due to insect pests, weeds and diseases

□ Insects   ▓ Diseases   □ Weeds

Annual yield loss world-wide because of weeds, diseases and insects as estimated by FAO, based on data pre 1990.

Source: Freeland, *Food for Life*, British Agrochemical Association

Contact herbicides affect *only the area of the plant that they are applied to*. Systemic herbicides are absorbed by plants, and are then transported to all parts of the plant through the phloem. This means that they can reach and kill *every part of the plant*. Another advantage of using systemic herbicides is that, once inside the plant, systemic herbicides are not affected by light (which can break down some contact herbicides) or rain (which can wash off contact herbicides).

Chemical control of insect pests

The use of pesticides (chemicals to protect crops from pests such as insects and fungi) is not new. Three thousand years ago, sulphur was used by the Greeks to kill pests, and the Chinese used arsenic in AD 900. More recently, naturally occurring chemicals such as nicotine from ground-up tobacco leaves, and pyrethrum from certain Kenyan daisies have been used. Since 1950, more than 500 chemical substances have been registered for use as pesticides in the UK. Some of these do not occur naturally but are made in laboratories. These are synthetic pesticides.

Like herbicides, insecticides can be broad-spectrum or specific. A broad-spectrum insecticide kills all insects with which it comes into contact, including beneficial species such as bees (which help to pollinate flowers) and ladybirds (which are voracious predators of insect pests such as aphids). So very careful timing is needed when applying a broad-spectrum insecticide, to try to limit its effects on beneficial insects. For example, you would not spray a broad-spectrum insecticide on an apple tree when it was in flower; if you did, you would kill the bees that visited the flowers, and so would get little or no crop of apples. Insecticides that target only a particular species are few and far between, and they are considerably more expensive than broad-spectrum ones.

Again like herbicides, insecticides can be classified as contact or systemic. Contact insecticides kill insects with which they make direct contact. Systemic insecticides are absorbed by the plant, and transported in the phloem. These are much more effective against sap-sucking insect pests such as aphids (greenfly) because every aphid that is feeding on the sap will be killed. A contact insecticide, however carefully sprayed onto

the plant, would be likely to miss many individual aphids.

Insecticides differ in their **persistence**. This is a measure of how quickly they break down. Many natural insecticides are quickly decomposed in the environment. Synthetic insecticides may not be decomposed as quickly (Fig. 11).

9 Suggest one advantage and one disadvantage of an insecticide that takes a long time to be broken down by decomposers.

When insecticides are not broken down, they may persist in food chains. As the chemicals pass from one trophic level to another, they become concentrated, particularly in fat deposits of top carnivores such as birds of prey. This is called bioaccumulation (see also the Minamata Bay case study, p. 27). The effect can be dramatic. For example, the broad-spectrum, persistent, fat-soluble insecticide **DDT** is now found in virtually all animal tissue, in every food chain, and even in Antarctic snow. At the kind of concentration in which it is applied to insects, DDT is not at all toxic to other animals. However, by the time it reaches the top carnivores in a food chain, the concentrations are high enough to weaken and possibly kill these animals.

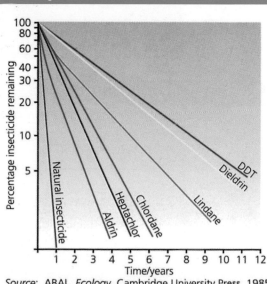

Fig. 11 Breakdown rate of insecticides

Source: ABAL, *Ecology*, Cambridge University Press, 1985

The first major use of DDT was in 1943, when it was used to kill body lice and halt the spread of a very unpleasant disease that they transmitted, called typhus. Since then, it has been widely used in many parts of the world to kill the mosquitoes that spread malaria. The World Health Organisation estimates that the use of DDT for these purposes has probably saved 25 million human lives. DDT is also used as an insecticide on crops such as cotton, to kill pests such as the cotton boll weevil. It was seen as the perfect insecticide – cheap to make, very toxic to insects but not to mammals, and very stable – so you only needed to spray a small amount in your house and there would be no mosquitoes for a very long time. Another persistent insecticide that came into use in the 1940s was dieldrin.

The 1950s decline in sparrowhawk and peregrine populations has been linked with the use of insecticides such as dieldrin and DDT (Fig. 12). These insecticides were used to treat cereal seeds before they were sown. They caused the death of many wildlife species, including long-tailed field mice, which are prey for sparrowhawks and peregrines. Table 8 shows results obtained by ecologists who trapped field mice and determined the concentrations of dieldrin and mercury in body residues. Two traps were used for four days before seeds treated with the chemicals were sown, and four traps for six days after the seeds had been sown.

There is evidence that the decline in peregrine populations resulted from a thinning of the shells of their eggs, making them less likely to develop and hatch. If the eggs fall below a certain mass they break during laying. In general, the egg shells were thinner in the intensively farmed south east compared with the north and west where DDT was less widely used. Experimental

The drop in wild populations of sparrowhawks in the UK began immediately after DDT started to be used in agriculture in 1946.

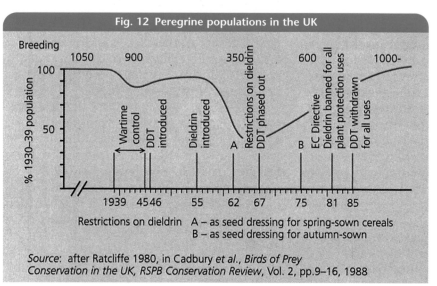

Fig. 12 Peregrine populations in the UK

Restrictions on dieldrin A – as seed dressing for spring-sown cereals
B – as seed dressing for autumn-sown

Source: after Ratcliffe 1980, in Cadbury et al., Birds of Prey Conservation in the UK, RSPB Conservation Review, Vol. 2, pp.9–16, 1988

Table 8 Long-tailed field mice					
Period	Trap	No. of mice caught	No. of mice analysed	Mean concentration of dieldrin/ parts per million (ppm) (wet mass)	Mean concentration of mercury compounds/ parts per million (ppm) (wet mass)
Before application	1	11	9	0.15	0.05
	2	15	4	0.23	0.03
After application	1	18	2	6.49	0.28
	2	18	7	10.96	0.41
	3	9	5	8.70	0.39
	4	12	5	12.06	0.42

Source: Jeffries et al., Journal of Zoology, vol. 171, pp. 513–539, 1973

evidence on captive birds of prey confirmed that DDT causes shell thinning in various species.

The use of DDT has been banned in Europe, including Britain, and in the USA, since the early 1970s, and a ban on its use in all parts of the world will probably come into effect in the early 21st century. Sparrowhawk and peregrine populations have risen and birds are returning to areas where they had disappeared. The amount of insecticide residues in their bodies has fallen, shell thickness has improved, the reproductive rate has increased, and survival has increased.

Another problem with the use of chemicals to kill insects is that populations that are resistant to the insecticide may evolve. All members of a pest species are not equally likely to be affected by a particular insecticide. Some individuals are genetically less susceptible and may survive to pass on their resistance to the next generation. This could lead to the development of significant pest resistance. Most insects have rapid reproductive rates, so the evolution of resistance can be quite quick (Fig. 13). With

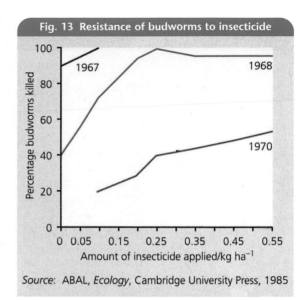

Fig. 13 Resistance of budworms to insecticide

Source: ABAL, *Ecology*, Cambridge University Press, 1985

female aphids, capable of breeding two weeks after birth, large numbers of resistant individuals could appear in the population in a single growing season. The more frequently an insecticide is used, the more likely resistance in the pest insect species is to evolve.

10a From Fig. 13, approximately how much insecticide achieved a 50% kill of budworms in: 1968; 1970?

b If the volume or concentration of insecticide has to be increased, what could be the effects on other species in the habitat?

The number of resistant species increases every year. By 1987, there were over 500 insect species, 150 plant disease-causing organisms and 50 weed species all resistant to the chemicals developed to kill them. Some species have developed resistance to more than one type of pesticide. Using different insecticides for the same insect pest can delay resistance development.

The development, manufacture and application of pesticides is now strictly regulated, and certain ideal characteristics are aimed for (Fig. 14). However, the environmental and long-lasting impact of pesticides must not be overlooked. They can cause harm to humans, and other beneficial animals and plants.

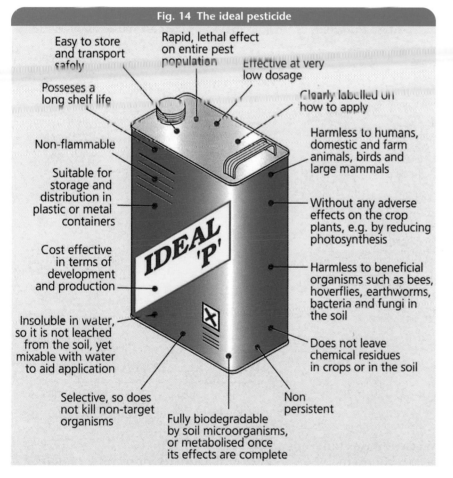

Fig. 14 The ideal pesticide

- Easy to store and transport safely
- Rapid, lethal effect on entire pest population
- Effective at very low dosage
- Possesses a long shelf life
- Clearly labelled on how to apply
- Non-flammable
- Harmless to humans, domestic and farm animals, birds and large mammals
- Suitable for storage and distribution in plastic or metal containers
- Without any adverse effects on the crop plants, e.g. by reducing photosynthesis
- Cost effective in terms of development and production
- Harmless to beneficial organisms such as bees, hoverflies, earthworms, bacteria and fungi in the soil
- Insoluble in water, so it is not leached from the soil, yet mixable with water to aid application
- Does not leave chemical residues in crops or in the soil
- Selective, so does not kill non-target organisms
- Non persistent
- Fully biodegradable by soil microorganisms, or metabolised once its effects are complete

IDEAL 'P'

4.5 Biological control of insect pests

Biological control involves the introduction of a natural predator or parasite, that will feed on the pest species and reduce its numbers. Biological control is an old idea. In the 13th century, Chinese farmers used to put ants on citrus trees to protect the trees from pests like aphids.

Introducing a predator to the pest reduces the level of the pest population by increasing the death rate. It does not get rid of the pest completely. Some pests must survive or the predator population would also die out.

11 Why do you think the numbers of pests fluctuate in Fig. 15, both before and after the introduction of control measures?

A biological control programme consists of the following stages:

- finding where the pest species comes from originally;
- finding predators of the pest, to become the control species;
- testing the control species to make sure no unwanted diseases are introduced and that only the target species is attacked;
- finding out whether the control is likely to work on a large scale;
- breeding or mass culture of the control species;
- releasing the control species;
- monitoring and evaluating the success of the programme.

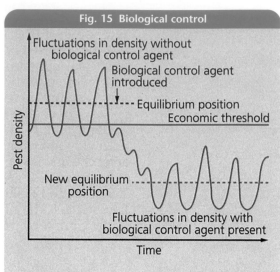

Fig. 15 Biological control

Fluctuations in density without biological control agent

Biological control agent introduced

Equilibrium position
Economic threshold

Pest density

New equilibrium position

Fluctuations in density with biological control agent present

Time

Source: *Biological Sciences Review*, Vol. 7, 1995

If properly chosen, biological control agents are very specific and attack only one pest, with few if any adverse effects on other organisms. Biological control can be cheaper than chemical insecticides if the control species can reproduce in the habitat where it is needed. Whereas the insecticide would need to be applied regularly, it is possible that just one introduction of the biological control agent will be sufficient to keep the pest numbers down to an acceptable level. A successful biological control method would replace the use of insecticides. The levels of insecticides in food chains and ecosystems would then fall.

CASE STUDY   **Biological control: success stories**

Some biological control species have been very successful. The prickly pear was an accidental introduction into Australia from America. It grew to be such a problem that it made 12 000 000 hectares of grazing land useless. The situation was brought under control by introducing the moth *Cactoblastis*. Its larvae bore holes into the prickly pear, allowing fungi to invade the cactus. It took only five years for the biological control to be successful.

Cottony cushion scale is an insect pest of citrus fruits in California and was controlled by the introduction of its native Australian predator, the ladybird.

Predatory mites are used commercially for control of red spider mites in glasshouses.

1 Why do you think biological control is most successful in enclosed areas such as glasshouses?

Integrated pest management

Biological control will not achieve the same level of pest control as use of chemical pesticides. Although many biological control products are being developed, they account for less than 1% of the total crop protection market. Biological control is unlikely to be the only control measure used. It often takes some time for the population of the control species to increase to such a level that it has an impact on the pest population level. In the meantime, a lot of crop damage may have occurred. Moreover, if pest numbers have built up to very high levels by the time the biological control agent is introduced, then it may prove impossible for the control species to have any significant effect on the pest population.

In many instances, a system of control measures has been worked out that uses both pesticides and biological control, as well as other methods such as the development of strains of crop plants that are naturally resistant to a particular pest. Such a system is called **integrated pest management (IPM)**. IPM can greatly reduce the quantity of pesticides that need to be used, so reducing costs for the farmer and possible harmful effects on plants or animals other than the pest species.

One example of the use of IPM is shown in Fig. 16. Leaf-roller caterpillars and red spider mites are important pests of apples. In this IPM programme, a combination of spraying with insecticide to kill the caterpillar, and using predatory mites to control the red spider mites, can be very successful.

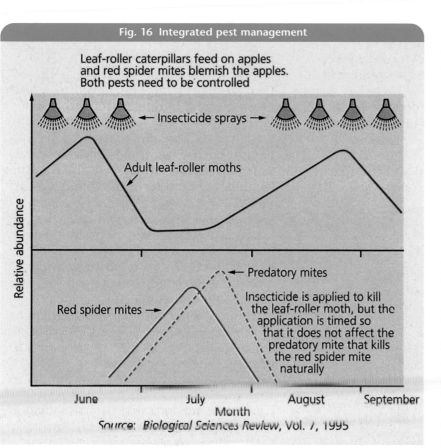

Fig. 16 Integrated pest management

Leaf-roller caterpillars feed on apples and red spider mites blemish the apples. Both pests need to be controlled

← Insecticide sprays →

Adult leaf-roller moths

Relative abundance

Red spider mites →

Predatory mites

Insecticide is applied to kill the leaf-roller moth, but the application is timed so that it does not affect the predatory mite that kills the red spider mite naturally

June   July   August   September
Month

Source: *Biological Sciences Review*, Vol. 7, 1995

- Competition with weeds and grazing by herbivores (including insects) can greatly reduce productivity of crop plants.

- Weeds can be controlled with herbicides, and insect pests can be controlled with insecticides. These may be broad-spectrum or specific, contact or systemic.

- An example of a selective herbicide is 2,4-D, which is a synthetic auxin that kills only broad-leaved plants.

- The persistence of a herbicide or pesticide is the length of time it takes to break down naturally.

- A persistent pesticide may build up in the bodies of animals as it travels along a food chain. This is called bioaccumulation. DDT and dieldrin are examples of insecticides that do this.

- Pests can evolve resistance to pesticides.

- Biological control involves introducing an predatory species to control the population of a pest species.

- Integrated pest management involves the use of a variety of appropriate control methods. It emphasises the use of natural factors such as predators, parasites and disease-causing organisms while restricting pesticide use to a minimum.

1 The diagram shows what happens to the light energy falling on a leaf.

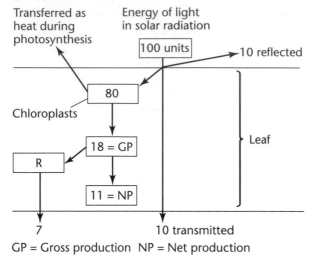

GP = Gross production NP = Net production
R = Respiration

a Give **one** way in which the structure of a leaf minimises the amount of light that is transmitted through it. (1)

b Calculate the percentage efficiency of photosynthesis in using the light absorbed by the chloroplasts for carbohydrate production. (1)

c Write an equation to show the relationship between gross production (GP), net production (NP) and respiration (R). (1)

NEAB BY07 February 1997 Q2

2

a Land use for crops of wheat and other cereals needs regular applications of fertilisers. Explain why fertilisers have to be added to this land each year. (1)

b Briefly describe how crop rotation can reduce the need for fertilisers. (2)

c The table shows a comparison of some features of organic and artificial fertilisers.

Feature	Organic fertilisers	Artificial fertilisers
Nutrient content	Variable	Constant
Solubility	Not immediately soluble	Soluble
Rate of release	Slow	Rapid
Concentration of ions in soil	Low	High
Bulk	Large	Small

Use the information in the table and your own knowledge to explain **three** advantages of using organic rather than artificial fertilisers. (3)

NEAB BY07 February 1997 Q1

3 Carbon dioxide is an essential raw material required by plants, but its concentration in the air is only about 0.03%. In a closed glasshouse carbon dioxide concentrations are often enriched. Carbon dioxide enrichment is normally carried out in the light and when vents are closed. Enrichment is only worthwhile for most crops during winter or early spring.

a Give **two** methods for enriching the carbon dioxide content of the air in glasshouses. (2)

b Explain why the concentration of carbon dioxide is **not** normally enriched to more than 0.1%. (2)

c Suggest why carbon dioxide enrichment is normally carried out only in winter or early spring. (2)

NEAB BY07 March 1999 Q2

4

a The graph shows the yield of a crop when different amounts of a nitrogen-containing fertiliser are applied.

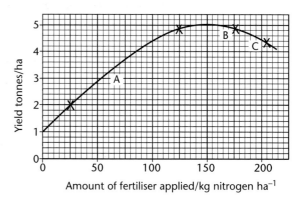

i) Explain the effect of the amount of fertiliser applied on the yield of the crop for each of the labelled sections of the curve. (3)

ii) A fertiliser costs 120p per kg nitrogen and the crop sells for £200 per tonne. Use the graph to calculate whether applying 125 or 150 kg nitrogen per hectare would be more profitable. Show your working. (2)

b Give **one** advantage and **one** disadvantage of using inorganic fertilisers instead of manure. (2)

NEAB BY07 June 2000 Q2

5 Dieldrin is an organochlorine pesticide. It was used to treat wheat grain before planting. An investigation was carried out to find the effect of treated wheat grain on the dieldrin concentration in the tissues of mice living in wheat fields. Mice were trapped before and after the treated wheat was planted. One line of traps was in the grass border of the field. The other was in the area planted with wheat.

The results are shown in the table on the right.

a i) Calculate the percentage change in mean dieldrin concentration in the tissues of mice from each of the two areas. Show your working. (2)
ii) Suggest **one** explanation for the different dieldrin content of mice trapped in the two areas after sowing. (1)

b Suggest **one** reason why the results of the investigation might be unreliable. (1)

c Suggest an explanation for the fact that the use of dieldrin is now banned in this country. (2)

NEAB BY07 March 1999 Q7

Period	Location of traps	No. of mice caught	No. of mice analysed	Mean dieldrin content of mice/ppm
Before sowing	In grass border	11	9	0.15
Before sowing	In planted area	15	4	0.23
After sowing	In grass border	18	2	6.49
After sowing	In planted area	18	7	10.96

6 The rhinoceros beetle is a pest which damages coconut palms growing on South Pacific islands. One method of control is to introduce a virus which kills the beetles. The virus was first used on the island of Tonga in 1971. The table below shows the results of surveys of rhinoceros beetle damage to palm trees carried out at two sites in 1971 and 1978

a The virus was introduced at sites A and B. At site A the virus was introduced as part of an integrated pest management scheme. Was the introduction of the virus more successful at site A or at site B? Support your answer with suitable calculations from the data in the table. (3)

b i) Suggest **two** techniques which could be combined with the introduction of the virus to produce effective pest management schemes. (2)
ii) Explain the benefits of an integrated pest management scheme. (2)

c Introduction of the virus is an example of biological control. Explain **two** possible limitations of biological control methods. (2)

NEAB BY07 June 1999 Q5

Site	1971		1978	
	No. of palm trees examined	No. of palm trees damaged by beetles	No. of palm trees examined	No. of palm trees damaged by beetles
A	289	48	302	23
B	226	34	278	28

When we catch fish from the open sea, we are acting as predators, and the fish are our prey. If we take too many fish, then their populations will drop so low that they are unable to recover.

Over-fishing is a global problem but here we will concentrate on the situation in the European Union (EU). In 1983, the EU introduced a Common Fisheries Policy, which included measures to limit fishing and conserve fish stocks. At the beginning of the 21st century, the problem of rapidly diminishing fish stocks has not gone away, and populations of some fish species, such as cod, are at dangerously low levels.

While sea fishing continues, albeit more and more tightly regulated, many countries – including Britain – are turning increasingly towards farming fish. This is known as **aquaculture**. In 1997, over 128 000 tonnes of fish and shellfish were produced in British fish farms, and this value continues to increase. However, this is a small amount compared with landings of wild sea fish and shellfish (which are actually crustaceans and molluscs), totalling nearly 900 000 tonnes in 1997. Moreover, aquaculture has its own set of problems, and is not an easy answer to saving the wild populations of fish in the seas around us.

By no means all of our food comes from agriculture. We obtain large quantities of food from the sea. When we do this, we act as hunter–gatherers, capturing wild animals that live their lives entirely out of our control.

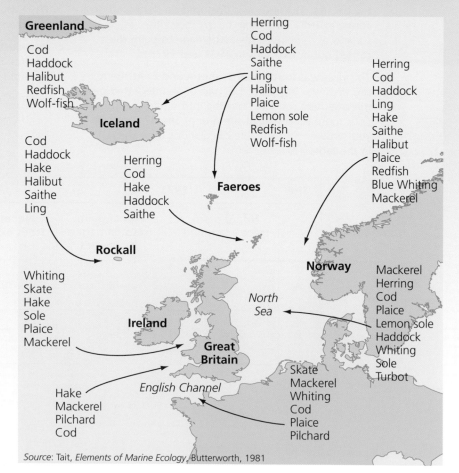

Greenland

Cod
Haddock
Halibut
Redfish
Wolf-fish

Iceland

Cod
Haddock
Hake
Halibut
Saithe
Ling

Herring
Cod
Hake
Haddock
Saithe

Faeroes

Herring
Cod
Haddock
Saithe
Ling
Halibut
Plaice
Lemon sole
Redfish
Wolf-fish

Herring
Cod
Haddock
Ling
Hake
Saithe
Halibut
Plaice
Redfish
Blue Whiting
Mackerel

Rockall

Whiting
Skate
Hake
Sole
Plaice
Mackerel

Ireland

Norway

North Sea

Mackerel
Herring
Cod
Plaice
Lemon sole
Haddock
Whiting
Sole
Turbot

Great Britain

English Channel

Hake
Mackerel
Pilchard
Cod

Skate
Mackerel
Whiting
Cod
Plaice
Pilchard

EU member states fish commercially in the north-east Atlantic, including the North Sea.

Source: Tait, *Elements of Marine Ecology*, Butterworth, 1981

5.1 Sustainable fishing

To ensure that we do not reduce fish populations to such low levels that they cannot recover, we need to understand what influences their population size. Data are collected about the numbers, sizes, sex ratios and ages of each species of fish in which we are interested, and these are used to try to work out how many fish, and what size of fish, we can take without endangering their populations in the long-term.

Fish populations

The **biomass** of a fish stock is the total mass of all living fish per unit volume or area, at a particular time (Fig. 1). The biomass of a population increases due to the growth of individual fish, and also **recruitment**.

Recruitment is the addition of new individuals that are either born into the population, or join it from elsewhere. The biomass of fish stocks decreases due to natural mortality and the effects of fishing.

A simple equation can be used to calculate the effects of these factors on the size of fish stocks:

$$S2 = S1 + (A + G) - (C + M)$$

where
$S1$ = biomass of stock at beginning of year
$S2$ = biomass of stock at the end of year
A = biomass of young fish added to stock
G = biomass added by growth of all fish in the stock
C = biomass caught by fishery
M = biomass lost through natural mortality.

If $S2 = S1$, then there is no net increase or decrease in biomass over the year. The population of that species of fish is stable.

What we would like to find is that $(A + G) - M$ is greater than zero. This would mean that the recruitment $(A + G)$ is greater than natural mortality. Assuming no fishing takes place (that is, C is zero), then the total biomass of the fish would actually *grow* during the year. The amount of this growth is known as the **natural yield**. It is a measure of productivity.

We can work out what biomass of fish we can take from that population, and still keep the population at a stable level. This amount is known as the **maximum sustainable yield**, or **MSY**. For the population of fish to remain stable, the biomass lost from the population $(C + M)$ must equal the biomass added $(A + G)$. The maximum sustainable yield is therefore $A + G - M$. If we take exactly this amount of fish, then we are removing the biomass of fish that equals the natural yield of the population. Taking fewer fish than this means that the biomass of the population will increase. Taking more fish means that the biomass of the population will decrease (Fig. 2 overleaf).

In practice, this is almost impossible to achieve, for a variety of reasons including the difficulty of collecting reliable data. Fish move around, so sampling in one place may tell you almost nothing about what is happening elsewhere. And even if we could collect enough data to put into the fishstock

Fig. 1 Biomass in a fish population

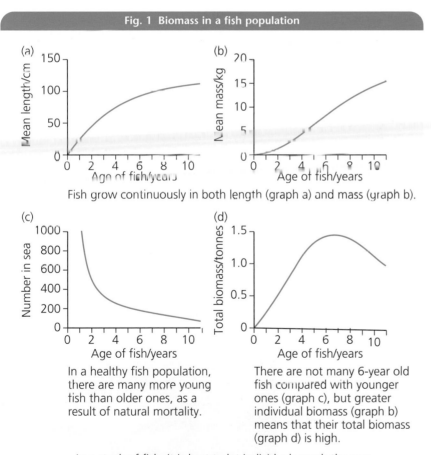

Fish grow continuously in both length (graph a) and mass (graph b).

In a healthy fish population, there are many more young fish than older ones, as a result of natural mortality.

There are not many 6-year old fish compared with younger ones (graph c), but greater individual biomass (graph b) means that their total biomass (graph d) is high.

In a stock of fish, it is best to let individuals reach the age of 6 years, so that they can breed for about three seasons before they are caught.

Source: adapted from Macer and Easey, *The North Sea Cod and the English Fishery Laboratory Leaflet 61*, MAFF, 1988

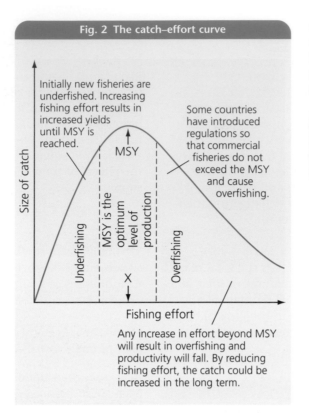

Fig. 2 The catch–effort curve

Initially new fisheries are underfished. Increasing fishing effort results in increased yields until MSY is reached.

Some countries have introduced regulations so that commercial fisheries do not exceed the MSY and cause overfishing.

Size of catch

MSY

MSY is the optimum level of production

Underfishing

Overfishing

X

Fishing effort

Any increase in effort beyond MSY will result in overfishing and productivity will fall. By reducing fishing effort, the catch could be increased in the long term.

equation on page 69, there is still the problem of ensuring that all the fishing fleets from all the countries that fish for this particular species will not, between them, take too many fish.

1 With reference to the equation on page 69, explain why, in the long term, a fishing effort greater than X in Fig. 2 will result in smaller catches.

KEY FACTS

- Fishing is an example of harvesting from a natural ecosystem.

- The natural increase of a fish population is known as the natural yield, and is a measure of productivity.

- A fish population will increase if the growth of individual fish, and the increase in numbers of fish

  in the population, outweigh the losses from mortality.

- Fishing can be sustainable if the total biomass of fish taken by fishing is not greater than the natural yield. This value is known as the maximum sustainable yield.

Fishing techniques

Worldwide, many different techniques are used to catch fish. They include the use of various types of nets, and also fishing with baited hooks attached to lines.

Trawling

Trawling is the most widely used fishing technique in the EU. Trawling catches fish that live on or near the sea bed. These are called **demersal fish**. In the north-east Atlantic, this includes cod, haddock, hake, whiting, plaice and sole. Trawling involves dragging a tapering bag of netting over the sea bed. There are two main types of trawl. The beam trawl (Fig. 3) has been used for hundreds of years and was the main type of trawl when vessels were sail-driven. Otter trawls (Fig. 4) are very efficient in the capture of demersal species and much larger nets can be used than with the heavier beam trawl. Modern trawlers

with a 750 kW engine can drag nets up to 100 m long. Plastic nets are stronger and lighter than nets made from natural fibres, and can therefore be much larger than the traditional nets. However, these nets are also rot-resistant and non-biodegradable; if lost overboard, they can trap marine mammals and damage other forms of marine life.

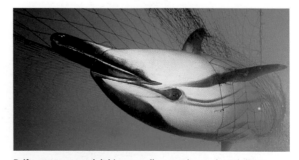

Drift nets can trap dolphins as wells as turtles, seals and diving birds. The animals cannot see the nets and may be lured by fish already caught in the them.

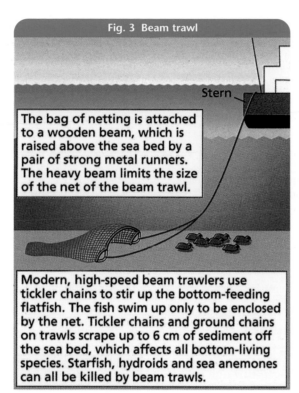

Fig. 3 Beam trawl

The bag of netting is attached to a wooden beam, which is raised above the sea bed by a pair of strong metal runners. The heavy beam limits the size of the net of the beam trawl.

Stern

Modern, high-speed beam trawlers use tickler chains to stir up the bottom-feeding flatfish. The fish swim up only to be enclosed by the net. Tickler chains and ground chains on trawls scrape up to 6 cm of sediment off the sea bed, which affects all bottom-living species. Starfish, hydroids and sea anemones can all be killed by beam trawls.

The target catch is the fish that are meant to be caught. But trawls are not selective and non-target fish often end up in the trawl. These fish can include fish of the wrong species, and fish that are too small. They are called the **by-catch** and are discarded. The by-catch is a significant threat to the conservation of some species. In 1987, the by-catch for North Sea haddock was estimated to be 41%.

Long-lining

Long lines can be used to fish in areas where the bottom is too deep or too rocky for trawlers. The length of the line may be as

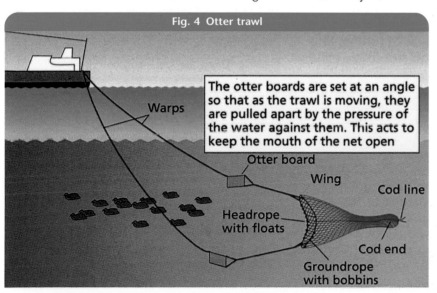

Fig. 4 Otter trawl

Warps

The otter boards are set at an angle so that as the trawl is moving, they are pulled apart by the pressure of the water against them. This acts to keep the mouth of the net open

Otter board

Wing

Cod line

Headrope with floats

Cod end

Groundrope with bobbins

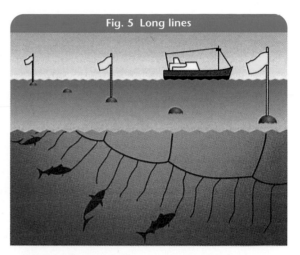

Fig. 5 Long lines

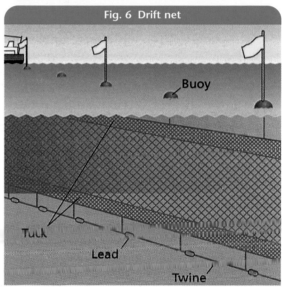

Fig. 6 Drift net

Buoy

Tuck

Lead

Twine

long as 100 km, with as many as 3000 baited hooks. Long lines can be used to catch either demersal or **pelagic** fish. Pelagic fish live in open water and swim in large groups called shoals. Pelagic long lines are buoyed up by floats at 300 m intervals (Fig. 5). Demersal long lines, with baited side lines, are anchored to the bottom of the sea bed and left for a couple of hours before hauling in.

Long lines can be made selective by the choice of bait and hook size. For example, relatively large hooks baited with squid are used to catch cod in the seas around Britain. The fish that are caught are handled individually, so they are sold in good condition and fetch a better price. This makes it a good technique for catching more expensive fish.

Drift netting

Drift nets (Fig. 6) are suspended by floats, and weighted at the bottom. They hang vertically in the water, usually measuring between 20 m and 30 m high. They can stretch from 5 to 50 km in length. Light, monofilament plastic drift nets are easier to handle and larger than natural fibre nets. Drift nets are used to catch pelagic shoaling species. Fish that try to swim through the nets become entangled by their gill covers. Drift nets can be made selective to some extent, by altering the mesh size. If the mesh is larger, smaller fish can swim through the net. Because of their danger to other animals, as well as their effect on fish stocks, the EU totally banned the use of drift nets for tuna fishing in the Atlantic and the Mediterranean, from 1 January 2002.

5.2 Regulating fisheries

In the EU, fishing is managed through the Common Fisheries Policy, or CFP. This was first introduced in 1983, and has been modified on several occasions since then.

One of the main aims of the CFP is to conserve fish stocks in waters fished by member countries of the EU. This is difficult to do because any regulations that reduce the quantity of fish caught will inevitably damage the livelihoods of people who depend, either directly or indirectly, on catching and marketing fish. Almost always, a compromise is reached between what the scientists say needs to be done, and what politicians think they can persuade their voters to accept.

Many countries have interests in the fish stocks in the north-east Atlantic. It is never easy to come to decisions that each member country of the EU sees as fair. The CFP uses a range of different measures to attempt to conserve fish stocks, while trying to take into account the economic and social aspects of fishing. These measures include allocating quotas, regulating mesh sizes, regulating the fishing effort, and imposing restrictions on where and when particular areas of the sea can be fished.

Quotas

The CFP states the maximum quantities of each species of fish that can be caught by EU member countries. This is known as the **total allowable catch** or **TAC**. To work this out, the maximum sustainable yield is first calculated, as explained on page 69. The TAC

High TACs have led to massive reductions in populations and catches of North Sea cod over the last 30 years.

should really be the same or less than the MSY, but this does not happen in practice for two main reasons. First, it is not easy to collect reliable data about the fish populations, so no-one is ever quite sure exactly what the MSY is. Secondly, political pressures are very great to make the TAC as large as possible.

Once the TAC is decided, it is shared out between member countries of the EU. This is done largely according to historical fishing patterns in each country, so as to keep the change for each country as small as possible. Each country's share of the TAC is called a **national quota**. This causes squabbling, as each member country feels that it is hard done by and that some other country is getting more than its fair share.

In late 2000, as a result of worrying statistics from scientists investigating fish population sizes, the EU ordered drastic

Table 1 Reductions in UK fishing quotas in the North Sea between 2000 and 2001		
Species	2000 quota/tonnes	2001 quota/tonnes
Haddock	53 045	41 780
Cod	34 360	18 930
Whiting	19 470	13 333
Plaice	1 450	1 170
Hake	270	160

reductions in quotas for five species of fish in the North Sea and to the west of Scotland (Table 1).

Cod used to be a very common fish, but it has been fished so heavily that numbers are now well below sustainable levels. In 1972, 300 000 tonnes of cod were caught in the North Sea. But in the year 2000, scientists from the Ministry of Agriculture, Fisheries and Food estimated that there were only 67 000 tonnes of breeding cod in the North Sea. They believe that, for the population to remain safe, this level should be close to 150 000 tonnes. The low stocks of cod in the North Sea meant that EU fishermen were not able to catch enough cod to reach the 81 000 tonne TAC in 1999.

To try to allow the cod population to recover, cod quotas have been cut. The British quota has been reduced by 45%, to just under 19 000 tonnes. This is almost certainly still too high, but fishermen's organisations were outraged at such a stringent cut. It represents a loss of about £60 million to Britain's fishing industry, and a probable loss of thousands of jobs.

As well as the difficulties in introducing quotas that are low enough to allow fish stocks to recover, there are also difficulties in making the quotas work. When trawling, fish of several different species may be caught in the net at once. In the North Sea, catches often include cod, haddock and whiting. If, for example, the fishing boat has already used up its quota for whiting, then it will have to throw them all back. Yet this will not help the whiting population, because the fish that have been caught will probably die.

> 2 With reference to Table 1, is it possible to predict for which species the reduction in quota between 1999 and 2000 is likely to have the greatest impact on the fishing community? Explain your reasoning. (HINT: start by calculating the percentage reduction in each quota.)

Net size restrictions

As well as ensuring that the total amount of fish caught is not too great, the CFP has also introduced a number of 'technical measures'. These aim to limit the capture of:

- small, immature fish;

- unwanted fish (those that have no commercial value or those for which the fishermen have already used up their quotas);

- other species, such as dolphins, turtles or birds.

It is important not to catch immature fish because this would greatly reduce the recruitment into the population (A + G) in the equation on page 69. Fish should be allowed to grow large enough to breed, and only caught when they are fully adult and have been able to lay eggs (spawn). For cod, it is best to let the fish live for 6 years before they are caught, so that they can breed for about three seasons. A female cod, if allowed to live for 10 years, can produce 76 million eggs. However, in 2000 it was estimated that the chance of a female cod living to this age in the North Sea was about the same as a person winning the National Lottery.

One important technical measure is the regulation of mesh sizes in the nets that are used. The idea is that small fish will be able to escape through the net, while larger ones will not. However, most nets have a mesh woven in diamonds, and these tend to close together as the net is pulled through the water. If a portion of the net is woven in squares, which stay open, the small fish have more opportunity to escape. The use of square-mesh panels was made compulsory when fishing for Norway lobsters and some other types of shellfish, where the by-catch of small fish tends to be particularly high.

Another difficulty is that different sizes of mesh are appropriate for different fish species. A relatively large mesh size is suitable for catching cod (which are large fish), while a much smaller mesh size is needed for catching mackerel. So a fishing boat might want to carry nets with different mesh sizes, to take advantage of whichever species they find. But this makes enforcement very difficult, because inspectors cannot be sure that the net with the smaller mesh has not been used for cod fishing.

In reality, the regulations have to be as straightforward and simple as possible, or they become unworkable. In 2000, the regulations on mesh sizes for towed nets in the seas around the EU were reviewed and made much simpler than they had previously been (Fig. 7).

3a Using Fig. 7, describe the two major differences in the minimum mesh size regulations imposed in 2000 compared with those in 1990.

b Suggest how these changes will make it more likely that the regulations will be followed.

c What effect are these changes likely to have on the number of very small fish that are caught?

Another measure to help reduce the chances of fish being caught before they are old enough to breed is the regulation of 'minimum landing sizes'. This regulation states the minimum size of fish, for each species, that can be brought into port and landed. Generally, these sizes match up with the sizes of nets that can be used in that area.

For some species, sizes have been increased, but for others they have been decreased. For example, in 2000 the minimum landing size for whiting was increased from 23 cm to 27 cm, while that for plaice was reduced from 27 cm to 22 cm.

Fishing effort

In 1993, when the CFP was 10 years old, it was decided that the regulation of mesh sizes and quotas was not preventing overfishing. There were far too many fishing vessels operating for the fish available. It was decided that fishing effort should also be reduced. Fishing effort is defined as the capacity (in tonnage or in engine power) of a fishing fleet multiplied by the number of days spent at sea. Since 1995, this has been regulated by issuing licences to all boats that fish in EU-regulated waters, and by issuing permits that state when and where they can fish.

Regulation of fishing effort is intended to conserve fish stocks, and to ensure that those who have licences to fish can earn a good living. If too many boats are fishing for too many hours, then not only are too many fish caught, but the number of fish caught by any one boat, and also their market value, will be

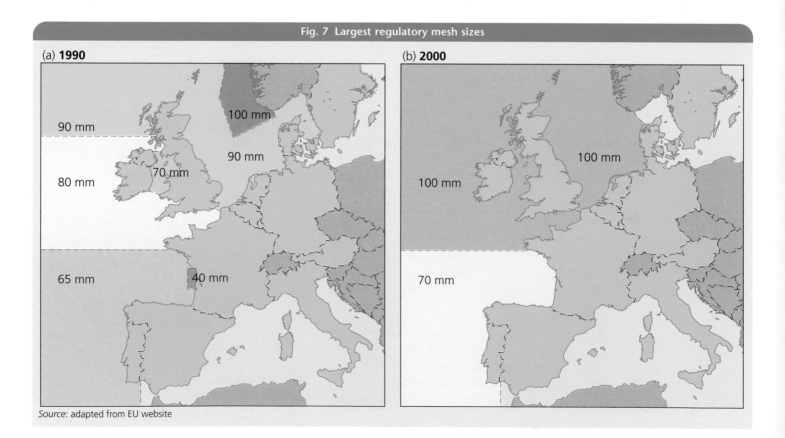

Fig. 7 Largest regulatory mesh sizes

(a) **1990**

90 mm
100 mm
90 mm
80 mm
70 mm
65 mm
40 mm

(b) **2000**

100 mm
100 mm
70 mm

Source: adapted from EU website

New fishing vessels are much more efficient than older ones. They may have new technology on board that makes it much easier to find shoals of fish, or have more efficient fishing gear. For the same fishing effort, many more fish will be caught by these newer boats than by older ones.

Fig. 8 Main spawning areas for plaice

■ Spawning area

February

March

Feb–March

Late January

Early January

Source: Tait, *Elements of Marine Ecology*, Butterworth, 1981

North Sea herring being prepared for landing at Great Yarmouth.

relatively small (Fig. 2 on page 70). Fishing effort can be reduced either by reducing the number of licences issued (so taking some fishing boats out of action completely) or by reducing the amount of time that each boat is allowed to spend at sea. Whichever is done, there will inevitably be hardship in communities that depend on fishing for their income.

Exclusion zones and closed seasons
Other measures that can be used to conserve fish stocks include completely banning fishing in particular areas, or at particular times of year. These regulations are intended to ensure that fish can breed successfully, and that young fish have a chance to grow to maturity and breed before they are caught. Spawning areas for particular species can be identified, and also areas (known as 'nurseries') where very small fish tend to congregate at particular times of year (Fig. 8). Fishing for that species in some of these areas at relevant times of year is banned.

Occasionally, fishing for a particular species may be completely banned for a period of time. In the late 1940s, very intensive trawling for North Sea herring developed. At that time, the stocks of herring were so vast that they were seen as inexhaustible. Huge numbers of herring, including very small ones, were caught and used to make cattle and poultry food. By the mid 1960s, the landings of herrings exceeded 3.5 million tonnes per year. However, landings fell dramatically in the next few years, an indication that the herring population had decreased. By 1976, catches had dropped to below 800 000 tonnes per year. Stocks had become so low that a total ban on all herring fishing throughout the north-east Atlantic, including the North Sea, was imposed. Even now, although recovery has been enough for herring fishing to be allowed again, the population of herring is nowhere near as great as in the 1940s.

KEY FACTS

■ The regulation of fisheries is intended to keep fishing for each species at or below the maximum sustainable yield. In the EU, this is done through the CFP.

■ Regulations in EU waters over the last 30 years have not been severe enough, nor sufficiently enforced, to prevent fish stocks from dwindling.

■ Quotas are imposed on each EU country, stating the total amount of each fish species that can be caught over one year.

■ Minimum net sizes are imposed, so that small fish can escape; this allows fish to reach breeding age before they are removed from the population.

■ Fishing effort (capacity of a fishing fleet × days spent at sea) is limited by the CFP.

■ Breeding areas and nursery areas for young fish are protected by regulations that limit fishing in these areas at certain times of year.

5.4 Fish farming

Fish farming has been taking place for a very long time. For example, medieval monasteries often kept fish ponds in which carp were grown for food. In recent years, there has been a significant increase in the quantity and range of fish that are produced by farming.

Fish and shellfish farming is known as aquaculture. In the EU, aquaculture comprises three main activities:
● farming of sea fish;
● farming of marine shellfish;
● farming of freshwater fish.

Table 2 shows the total tonnage of fish and shellfish produced by aquaculture in 1997. In the mid 1990s, the quantity of fish produced globally by fish farming was about a quarter of the quantity of fish caught at sea.

4 Using the information in Tables 1 and 2, suggest why fish farming in the UK is unlikely to have a large effect on the sea fishing industry.

Table 2 Aquaculture in 1997			
Species	**World production/ tonnes**	**Production in the EU/ tonnes**	**Production in the UK/ tonnes**
Salmon	523 213	115 749	99 197
Trout	436 592	235 541	15 100
Carp	8 006 325	18 264	0
Eels	8 134	8 053	0
Sea bass and bream	67 968	46 136	0
Turbot	3 220	3 220	75
Mussels	732 928	514 507	12 991
Oysters	3 085 118	97 876	1 053
Clams	1 332 729	49 670	36

Advantages of fish farming

Benefits of fish farming, as compared with fishing for wild stocks, include:

- a controlled supply of specific fish of the required size available independent of external conditions;
- achieving an optimum growth rate, health and palatability;
- a controlled genetic selection for desired qualities such as disease resistance.

It might be thought that if we can increase the amount of fish produced under controlled conditions, then we will not want to catch so many fish from the open sea. However, people seem to want to eat more and more fish. This may be because of moves towards more 'healthy eating', as fish is a low-cholesterol high-protein food. Moreover, many people have moved away from eating red meat because of scares such as BSE. So, although the quantity of fish produced by aquaculture is increasing, the demand for fish is increasing at at least the same rate and aquaculture is, as yet, having little if any effect on the demand for fish caught at sea.

Fish farming has benefits when compared with farming other animals, such as poultry, cattle, sheep or pigs. Fish are very efficient at converting food into biomass. This is because they are ectothermic – unlike birds and mammals, they do not use energy from the food they eat to maintain their body temperature. This means that they can use a greater proportion of their food to increase body mass.

Systems of fish farming

Fish farming has existed for many centuries, particularly in warmer parts of the world. Developments from early, primitive methods of aquaculture have given rise to various systems. These fall into two main categories.

Open systems

Open systems (also called extensive systems) employ natural production under near-natural conditions. For example, fast-growing fish such as carp are taken from a local river and placed in ponds. Animal manure is used as fertiliser to promote the growth of pondweed, which not only provides food for the herbivorous fish, but also oxygenates the water. The extensive system results in high productivity (Fig. 9 overleaf). Along with the low food and labour costs, it ensures a highly profitable form of aquaculture.

In open system fish farming, the minimum of management is necessary, though some effort may be made to reduce mortality by controlling competitors and predators.

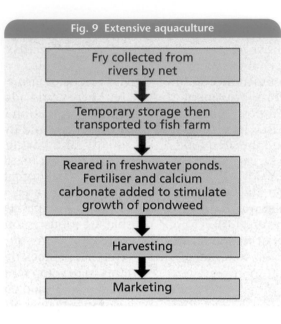

Fig. 9 Extensive aquaculture

Fry collected from rivers by net

↓

Temporary storage then transported to fish farm

↓

Reared in freshwater ponds. Fertiliser and calcium carbonate added to stimulate growth of pondweed

↓

Harvesting

↓

Marketing

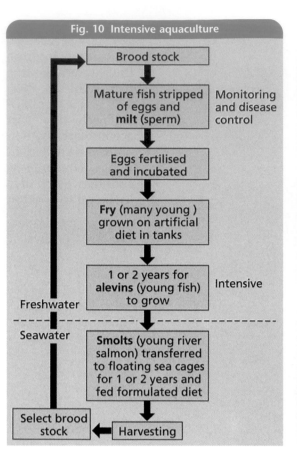

Fig. 10 Intensive aquaculture

Brood stock

↓

Mature fish stripped of eggs and **milt** (sperm) — Monitoring and disease control

↓

Eggs fertilised and incubated

↓

Fry (many young) grown on artificial diet in tanks

↓

1 or 2 years for **alevins** (young fish) to grow — Intensive

Freshwater

- -

Seawater

↓

Smolts (young river salmon) transferred to floating sea cages for 1 or 2 years and fed formulated diet

↓

Select brood stock ← Harvesting

Closed systems

Closed systems (also called intensive systems) are not usually natural systems. Fish, such as salmon or trout, are kept at high densities usually in cages in lakes or the sea, and measures are taken to ensure that they grow as quickly and efficiently as possible to a marketable size (Fig. 10). The type and

quantity of food provided is carefully regulated to match the different stages in the growth of the fish, and chemicals may be added to the water to control disease.

In closed systems, the breeding of the fish is tightly controlled. For example, in trout farming, day-length may be artificially manipulated to induce spawning at times of year when breeding would not normally take place. Fish that are to be used for breeding are kept separately from those that are to be harvested, and are fed on a special diet that increases the quantity and quality of eggs. Females are stripped of their eggs by stroking their abdomens, and males stripped of their sperm in a similar way. Eggs and sperm are mixed and incubated under controlled temperature conditions. Water flows constantly over the developing eggs, to ensure good oxygenation. During the latter part of the incubation period, the developing eggs can be safely transported, for example to another trout farm. Particular trout farms may specialise either in breeding fish, or in growing them on to harvestable size.

Salmon farming in a Scottish sea loch.

CASE STUDY Potential environmental effects of the salmon farming industry

Fish farming is a young industry, and we still do not really know the full effects that it may be having on the environment. At the beginning of the 21st century, many people are increasingly concerned that these effects may be widespread and serious. They include a possible reduction in the genetic diversity of wild salmon, a serious decrease in numbers of wild salmon, *Salmo salar*, and a reduction in species diversity in the sea lochs where salmon farming is taking place.

Effects on wild salmon populations

Wild salmon reproduce in freshwater rivers. They spend 2–3 years there before making the journey to the sea. After spending a year or so at sea, they return to the river where they were born to breed. This has helped to produce considerable genetic diversity among wild salmon, because the population in one river does not freely interbreed with those in another river. In contrast, farmed salmon have been selected to be of a particular type, and inbreeding among these fish has produced considerable genetic uniformity. If these farmed fish escape – and many do – and interbreed with wild fish, this is likely to reduce the genetic diversity of wild populations.

The Atlantic salmon is also farmed on the west coast of Canada. Here, the problem of escaped fish is potentially very harmful to the populations of other species of salmon that are native to the Pacific Ocean. Escaped Atlantic salmon will compete with the native salmon, and may reduce their numbers significantly.

Populations of wild salmon on the west coast of Scotland appear to be falling drastically. This has been happening for some time, and there are likely to be a number of different reasons. However, it does seem that increased parasite infestation resulting from salmon farming is at least partly responsible.

Farmed salmon are kept in cages in very high densities; this increases the risk of their being affected by diseases and parasites. A major parasite of both farmed and wild salmon is the sea louse, which attaches to the skin of the fish and feeds on it. Research has shown that wild fish that are heavily infested with sea lice are much less likely to survive than unparasitised fish. Even though salmon farmers try to reduce sea lice infestations, mainly by the addition of chemical treatments to their feed, there are still high concentrations of sea lice and their larvae in lochs where salmon farming takes place. As wild salmon leave their freshwater rivers and swim out to sea, they pass through these lochs and seemingly pick up much heavier infestations of sea lice than is normal. This may help to explain why researchers have found that, in recent years, only a tiny fraction of the wild salmon that leave a river ever return to it. Some Scottish rivers appear to have completely lost their salmon populations.

Effects on other species

Research carried out on the east coast of Canada has shown that, at least in areas where water movements are relatively sluggish, the build-up of faeces and waste food from fish farming has long-term effects on the community of bottom-living animals. Species are lost from this community, reducing biodiversity, and the relative abundance of species that remain changes greatly. These effects do not appear to be quickly or easily reversible.

Salmon farming also has very considerable effects on the populations of fish that live far from the fish farms. Salmon are carnivores; they need to eat animal material. The food pellets that they are given are made from other fish – such as capelin and sand eels that are caught in the Atlantic. About one-third of the fish that are caught each year are turned into fish oil or fish meal for feeding farmed livestock; around 30% of this is used for feeding farmed salmon. This is very inefficient; about 3.5 kg of wild fish are required to produce 1 kg of farmed salmon.

Reducing these harmful effects

Nowadays, a licence to start a fish farm depends on an environmental impact plan. Regulation of the size, stocking density and siting of fish farms can help to reduce the effects of pollution from fish faeces and waste food. However, tighter regulations are probably required to reduce sea lice infections and the problems caused by escaped fish.

Another positive move has been to develop carefully calculated 'high energy, low pollution' diets for the farmed fish, which minimise waste and hence pollution. Timing of feeding so that fish are ready to eat all that they are given can also help, as can using some method of removing uneaten food and faeces before they are swept out into open water. Another way of reducing this pollution is to use **polyculture**. Here, instead of farming a single species, the fish farm grows fish, shellfish such as mussels (which are filter feeders) and algae all together. This not only reduces effluents, but can also increase the total amount of biomass that is produced in a particular area.

The quantity of pesticides used can be minimised if good hygiene is practised. In many areas, stocking densities have been reduced to allow plenty of clean water to flow through the fish cages. This reduces the incidence and severity of disease and hence the need to use pesticides. As in agriculture, 'crop rotation' can help – in this case it involves keeping different kinds of fish in a particular place in successive years. This decreases the chance of a particular pathogen that infects a particular species from building up to dangerous levels. It can also be helpful to have 'fallow' years during which a cage is left entirely empty.

1 Explain how polyculture can reduce adverse effects on the environment.

■ Fish farming, unlike fishing, can produce fish of a particular species and size under controlled conditions.

■ Fish are very efficient at converting food into fish biomass, as they are exothermic and do not use energy to maintain their body temperature.

■ Open or extensive aquaculture involves keeping fish under relatively natural conditions.

■ Closed or intensive aquaculture involves keeping

fish in more controlled conditions, for example in cages in a sea loch, or inside a building in which temperature and lighting can be regulated.

■ Waste food or faeces from fish farms can cause eutrophication. Pesticides used to control disease in farmed fish can be very harmful to other organisms.

■ Polyculture can reduce the harmful impact of fish farms on other organisms.

1

a Give **two** differences between an intensive and an extensive system of fish farming. (2)

b Young fish, each weighing 2 g, were used to stock a series of tanks at different densities. The table shows the effect of stocking density on the growth rate of the fish.

No. of fish per tank	Growth rate/g per fish per day
250	0.032
500	0.026
750	0.020
1000	0.014
1500	0.008

Explain the effect of stocking density on the growth rate of the fish. (2)

c On a freshwater fish farm, tanks may be built at different levels so that water falls from tank to tank. The water is then recycled.
   i) Explain the advantage of letting water fall from tank to tank. (1)
   ii) Suggest **one** disadvantage of using recycled water. (1)

NEAB BY07 June 2000 Q5

2 The drawings give information about two methods of catching fish in oceans.

a Drift netting was used extensively to catch tuna fish in the Pacific Ocean until it was banned in 1991. The nets often reached 50 km in length. Give **two** reasons why this method of fishing was banned. (2)

Drift netting

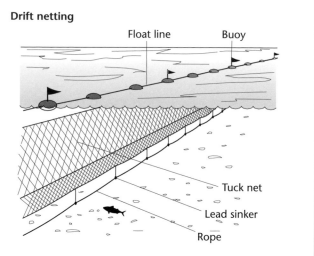

(Reproduced by permission of the *New Scientist*)

Long line hook fishing

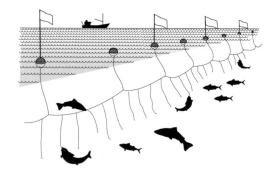

(Reproduced by permission of the University of Washington)

b Long lines for ocean fishing often reached 80 km in length. Although long line fishing is not banned in oceans it is no longer used extensively except in certain parts of the developing world. Suggest and explain the reason for this. (2)

NEAB BY07 June 1999 Q1

3 The drawing gives information about beam trawling.

> The runners are pulled along the sea bed. The tickler chains disturb fish living on the bottom. The trawl, weighing 5000 kg, digs deep into the sea bed.

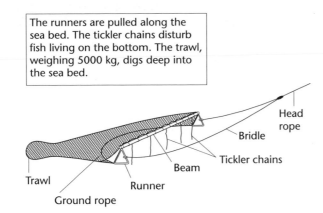

a Using information from the drawing, explain **two** ways in which beam trawling may damage marine ecosystems. (4)

b In recent years the size and engine power of trawlers have increased considerably. Explain **one** possible effect of this on fisheries. (2)

NEAB BY07 March 1999 Q1

4
a Explain how the use of a drift net differs from the use of a trawl net. (1)

b The graph shows the percentage of fish of different sizes caught in trawl nets with four different mesh sizes.

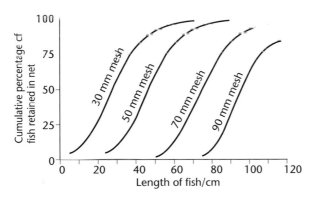

i) The minimum length of fish which can be legally caught is 50 cm. Give the mesh size which should be used and why. (2)
ii) Give **two** reasons for allowing fish below a minimum size to escape. (2)

c The graph shows three different stocks of the same species of fish.

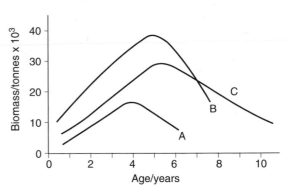

Which curve, **A**, **B** or **C**, is most likely to represent an overfished stock? Give **two** reasons for your answer. (3)

NEAB BY07 June 2000 Q3

5
a Describe how natural factors affect the productivity of a sea fishery. (3)

b In many areas, such as the North Sea, fish populations have been severely reduced by over-fishing. Explain what would happen to the fish population in an over-fished area
i) if fishing were totally banned for several years; (2)
ii) if the permitted mesh size of nets were increased. (2)

c The graph shows the net recruitment for one species of fish in a fishery at different population sizes. Net recruitment is the increase in number of fish per year.

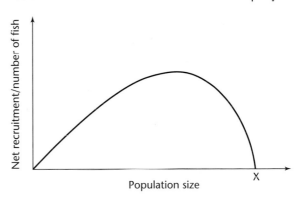

i) Explain why net recruitment decreases as the population size approaches **X**. (2)
ii) Mark clearly on the graph with an M the population size that provides the maximum yield in this fishery. Explain your answer. (3)

NEAB BY07 February 1997 Q9

6 Conservation

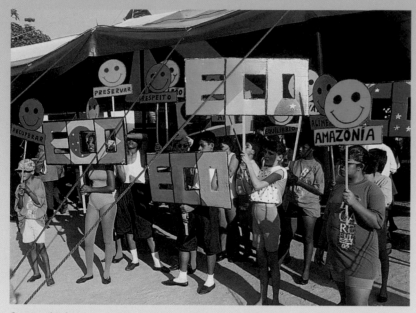

Conservation issues motivate many people. This demonstration took place at the 1992 Earth Summit in Rio de Janeiro, Brazil (p. 90).

The impact of humans on the environment has increased enormously over the last few centuries. This has happened because of human population growth, and our ever-increasing exploitation of resources in the environment. We have cleared forests and drained wetlands to provide land for agriculture, buildings and transport links. Intensive farming has transformed habitats. Increases in demands for energy have meant that more and more fossil fuels have been burnt, releasing into the atmosphere gases that have resulted in acidification of rain, and that may result in global warming.

As these problems have grown, so has people's awareness of the damage we are doing. Increasingly, many people want to do something to prevent further harm. The first wildlife protection laws in Britain came into effect in the 19th century, and since then there has been a steady increase in legislation that attempts to protect species and habitats in the UK. Non-governmental environmental groups are increasing in number, size and effectiveness. And international agreements between governments of many countries have attempted to solve some of the major global problems such as the damage to the ozone layer and global warming.

All of these efforts to prevent further harm to the environment, and efforts to try to reverse the harm we have already done, come under the broad heading of 'conservation'. In this chapter, we will look at examples of conservation that range in scale from local to global.

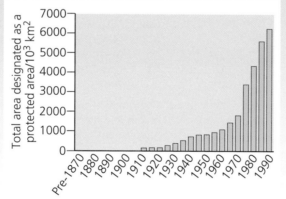

Globally, more and more land is coming under some type of environmental protection.

Source: Mather and Chapman, *Environmental Resources*, Longman Scientific and Technical, 1995

6.1 ## Principles of conservation

The fundamental aim of conservation is to maintain or increase biodiversity. Biodiversity is a difficult term to define. It can be considered as the variety of different living organisms and environments that there are on Earth. This includes:

- ecosystems;
- species;
- genetic diversity within each species.

Conservation, therefore, attempts to ensure that we do not allow the number and range of different ecosystems or species, or the genetic diversity within species, to decline.

Reasons for conservation

For many people today, the reasons for conservation are moral and ethical. This means that conservation should be undertaken for its own sake as a fundamental duty to protect the variety of species and habitats on Earth, which humans have no right to spoil or endanger.

This view, however, has only become common in the UK in the last two hundred years or so. Previously, most people in the UK would have seen the Earth's resources as materials to exploit. Such a view may still be common today in many developing countries. Where people are living under hard conditions, struggling to feed themselves and to survive, then conservation is a luxury they cannot even begin to contemplate, however much they love and enjoy the biodiversity that surrounds them. If people from richer countries want conservation to be undertaken in such places, then they have to try to understand the views of local people.

Conservation can, however, have positive economic outcomes. For example, more than 40% of medical prescriptions in the USA contain one or more ingredients that originated from wild plant species. Conserving species diversity of plants could result in the discovery of new drugs, bringing economic benefits to some people and health benefits to others. Plant breeding programmes to produce new crop varieties often use genes in wild varieties of plant. Conserving genetic diversity of plant species could bring economic benefits to the plant breeders and to the farmers who grow the plants.

Conservation programmes

Before conservation can begin, we need as much information as possible about what we are trying to conserve. Imagine, for example, that a small woodland has been recognised as an important wildlife habitat, and that an environmental organisation wants to conserve it. They would first need to sample and collect data about the species present (see Chapter 1), and about the abiotic characteristics in the woodland. They would need to identify which species or features are most under threat, and identify the threats as precisely as possible. It would also be helpful to monitor the woodland over time to look for any changes that may be taking place in the community. Armed with this information, the environmental organisation could then draw up a management plan that stated the aims of the conservation programme, and gave details of how to carry it out, including sources of funding.

You might think that a better way of conserving such a woodland would be to put a strong fence around it to keep everyone out, and then just to leave it alone. Cases where such an approach is useful are relatively rare. The 'leave it alone' method is most likely to maintain biodiversity if the area is truly wild and untouched by humans. Such wildlands do still exist in places; for example, deep in the Amazonian rainforests in some parts of

The chalk downlands of southern Britain, with their wonderfully rich range of flowering plants, are the result of forest clearance centuries ago, and grazing by sheep.

Brazil, some of the rainforests in Papua New Guinea, the hearts of deserts such as the Sahara and the icy lands of Antarctica. But even here, pressures from forestry and mining make it difficult to be sure that these special places will remain so in the future.

In many cases, what we want to conserve is something that is the result of previous human activity. Many of the habitats that we think of as special only exist because human activity has prevented them from undergoing succession. If we stop grazing sheep on downlands, or stop clearing out silt from freshwater ponds, they will undergo succession and end up as woodland. The woodland in our example above may contain species that would be lost if we allowed natural succession to occur. Conservation is almost always an active process.

One principle that has emerged as more and more conservation programmes are introduced is the necessity to involve local people. It simply does not work for an outside organisation to force conservation measures on people who live on the land, and who depend on it for their livelihoods. Conservation projects are most likely to succeed if local people are directly involved or obtain some benefit. In a country such as the UK, where most people have relatively comfortable lives with plenty to eat, medical care and good housing, the benefit may be simply the enjoyment of seeing a habitat maintained and not spoilt. In a developing country, the benefit may need to be more material. For example, efforts to conserve elephants in Zimbabwe were not initially very successful. Poaching of elephants for their ivory was common, and local people resented the damage that elephants did to their crops. However, the introduction of a project called

Campfire had a very positive effect on the elephant conservation programme. Local people are now involved in the management programme, and local communities are able to make money from allowing hunters to shoot some of the elephants. This may sound as though it is exactly the opposite to what is required, but the number and age of the elephants that are killed are carefully chosen, so that there is no harm to the population as a whole. The people who share their habitat with elephants now have a sound financial reason to help to conserve them.

Different aspects of conservation
The focus of a conservation programme may be very narrow, or very broad. Such programmes may concentrate on one or more of the following:
- **species conservation** – focused on saving particular species from extinction;
- **nature conservation** – focused on maintaining a variety of habitats in a particular area;
- **biological conservation** – focused on maintaining species diversity within a habitat;
- **environmental conservation** – focused on maintaining the abiotic factors in an ecosystem;
- **global conservation** – focused on developing international cooperation in worldwide projects such as maintaining the composition of the atmosphere.

These programme categories are not sharply divided. Many, if not most, conservation programmes involve at least two of them. In the remainder of this chapter, we will look at each type of programme, considering its special features as well as the general conservation principles that they all share.

6.2 Species conservation

We have no idea how many different species there are on Earth. About 1.5 million species have been identified, but all the time we are discovering more. Even large organisms, such as mammals or trees, are still being newly discovered. Take into account all of the less noticeable organisms, such as unknown bacteria and insects, and some biologists estimate that the true number of species is probably at least 5 million and could be as many as 80 million.

Captive breeding

Wherever possible, species conservation should involve habitat conservation. Everyone agrees that the best place for a species to live is in its natural habitat. In Britain, laws protect certain species from disturbance – for example, bat roosts must not be disturbed, and ponds in which great crested newts breed cannot be destroyed without permission.

However, protecting species within their natural environment is not always possible – or, at least, not straight away. If the population size of a species has dropped to such low levels that it is thought unlikely to survive in the wild, then a **captive breeding programme** may be introduced. Zoos and botanic gardens around the world may become involved in such a programme, with the aim of building up numbers of the species while attempts are made to rescue and conserve its natural habitat. Eventually, it may be possible to return the species to the wild.

Such breeding programmes try to maintain genetic diversity within the population. If closely related animals are bred together, then the degree of genetic variation within the population is likely to decrease. Breeding between closely-related individuals is called **inbreeding**, and it increases the risk that an individual will receive the same harmful, recessive allele from both its parents. Reduction of genetic diversity within a population increases the risk of disease. So, a zoo in one part of the world may 'borrow' an animal from another zoo, in order to create a breeding pair that are as genetically different from one another as possible. Breeding between animals with different genotypes is called **outbreeding**. If the animals themselves cannot easily be moved, or if they are reluctant to mate in the environment provided for them by the zoo, then artificial insemination may be used.

Sometimes, the numbers of an endangered species are so small that there are not enough healthy females for a viable breeding programme using conventional breeding procedures. In such instances, eggs and sperm may be obtained from a male and female, and placed together *in vitro* for fertilisation to occur. The resulting embryos are then placed in the uterus of a female animal of a different but closely-related species, who acts as a surrogate mother.

1 How can the use of surrogate mothers speed up results in a captive breeding programme for a species of large mammal such as an antelope?

It is easiest to raise money for species that people find appealing. These are almost always large mammals, such as tigers, giant pandas, white rhinos and snow leopards – like this one – rather than, say, a rare slug or plant.

CASE STUDY — **The Millennium Seed Bank and the St Helena Boxwood**

Scientists at the Royal Botanic Gardens at Kew have been collecting and storing seeds since 1974. The Millennium Seed Bank is a new and ambitious project, which opened in 2000 and provides better facilities for storing seeds from many more species. Its aims are:

- to collect and conserve representative samples of the 1400 native British plants that set seed;
- to collect and conserve seeds from 10% of the world's flora (seeds from more than 24 000 species), concentrating on plants that grow in dry places in the tropics and sub-tropics.

The Seed Bank opened just in time to play a major role in saving the St Helena boxwood from extinction. St Helena is a small island in the South Atlantic Ocean, thousands of miles from the nearest mainland in southern Africa. Like many isolated islands, it has a number of species that have evolved there, and are found nowhere else in the world. The St Helena boxwood, *Mellissia begoniifolia*, is one such species. First described in 1875, when it was already very rare, the St Helena boxwood was thought to be extinct by the mid 20th century. In 1999, a single remaining plant was found. It looked as though it was dying.

The last plant on St Helena has now died and *Mellissia* is truly extinct in the wild. Hopes rest on the 53 plants like this one growing in controlled conditions.

Scientists from Kew and from St Helena worked hard to try to save this species. They took cuttings from the plant, but none of them rooted. None of the seeds lying in the soil around the plant germinated. It looked as though, having been rediscovered at the last minute, the boxwood was about to become *genuinely* extinct.

Eventually, about 400 seeds from the dying plant and the soil around it were collected. They were shared out between several different organisations, in the hope that at least someone would manage to persuade some to germinate. And this has resulted in success. By 2001, there were 5 plants on St Helena, 2 at the Royal Horticultural Society at Wisley in Surrey, and 46 at Kew. Of those 46 plants, 38 have been grown from seed and 8 propagated from cuttings.

Studies of the genome of the individual *Mellissia* plants have been made at Kew and it has been found, not surprisingly, that there is virtually no genetic variation between the plants. This is not good news for *Mellissia*, because without genetic variation it is not possible for the plant to adapt to changes in its environment. It is likely that the lack of genetic variation results from almost all of the individuals of this species having died some time ago – all the seedlings that are now growing have inherited their genes from a single parent plant.

Nevertheless, there is still hope that *Mellissia* can eventually be returned to the wild. The original seedlings grown at Kew flowered in September 2000, and hand pollination resulted in a number of fruits being produced. The first 35 ripe fruits were harvested in January 2001, each containing 20–40 seeds. These have all been sent to the Millennium Seed Bank, where they will be kept safely in store, in the hope of eventual repatriation to St Helena.

1 Suggest what needs to be done before attempts are made to return plants of the St Helena boxwood to the wild in St Helena.

Thanks to Dr Wolfgang Stuppy and the Royal Botanic Gardens, Kew.

CASE STUDY

The scimitar-horned oryx

The scimitar-horned oryx, *Oryx dammah*, was once widespread in the semi-deserts of Northern Africa. Local people have always used it as a source of meat and skins, but with the development of modern firearms the number killed by hunters increased dramatically. Employees of oil and mineral companies based in this area hunted the animals for pleasure, as did soldiers involved in a long-running war in northern Chad. By the 1960s, it was recognised that the oryx was in imminent danger of extinction, and it is now listed in the International Union for Conservation of Nature (IUCN) Red List of Threatened Animals.

During the 1960s and 1970s, several oryx were caught and transported to zoos in Europe, Russia and the USA. They have readily bred in captivity, and there are now more than 2000 of them in zoos in more than 50 countries. One of these zoos is Marwell Zoological Park, near Winchester in Hampshire. This zoo was founded in the 1970s with the particular aim of being an ark for endangered species. It is now one of the world's leading zoos in the breeding of endangered species. Almost all of the animals kept at Marwell have been captive-bred.

In the early 1970s, a programme was set up with the aim of reintroducing the oryx to its natural environment. The programme followed guidelines laid down by IUCN for captive breeding and reintroduction programmes, and it took place in three stages. Stage 1 established breeding centres, Stage 2 involved the setting up of wildlife reserves in the area where the animals had originally lived in the wild. Stage 3 was the selection and release of 10 zoo-bred oryx to this reserve.

Ten animals were transported to the first reserve in Tunisia in 1985. They were initially kept in holding pens. Later, they were moved to larger acclimatisation pens, where they grazed on the natural vegetation. Finally – 20 months later – they were released into the 1500 hectare reserve. By 2000, the original 10 animals had grown to a population of more than 120.

In 1999, another group of oryx was released into a second, larger reserve, still in Tunisia. This 6135 hectare area of desert steppe was first fenced for six years to keep out grazing livestock, giving time for the vegetation to recover from previous overgrazing. The reintroduction programme was carried out by Marwell Zoo and Bratislava Zoo working closely together. The animals that were released came from six zoos in five countries, so ensuring that they were as genetically diverse as possible.

The maintenance of genetic diversity in the oryx populations has been a central focus of this captive breeding programme. Marwell Zoo keeps a stud book (a history of the relationships between individual animals) for all the oryx in zoos in Europe. This can be used – with the aid of a computer program – to plan which animals should be bred with which in order to retain the maximum possible genetic diversity within the oryx population. If genetic diversity is lost, then it becomes very difficult for the species to adapt to any changes in its environment, lessening the chance of its future survival.

1 a Explain why it is important that the people of Tunisia, especially those living near to the reserves, are supportive of the reintroduction project.

b Suggest what can be done to increase this local support.

Thanks to Marwell Zoological Park, Winchester.

Hundreds of scimitar-horned oryx have been bred at Marwell over the last 30 years.

CITES

In 1973, one hundred and forty-five countries signed an agreement that controls international trade in endangered species and products from them such as ivory. This agreement is called the Convention on International Trade in Endangered Species of Wild Fauna and Flora, or CITES.

CITES lists species under different Appendices. Species in Appendix I are those that are threatened with extinction, and all commercial trade in these species is banned. Exceptions may be granted if the animal or plant is being moved from one country to another for research purposes, or for a captive breeding programme, or if the animal or plant has been bred in captivity or propagated by tissue culture. Species included in Appendix I include tigers, rhinos, sea turtles, some orchids and some cacti.

Appendix II species are those which, while not immediately threatened with extinction, may become so if trade in them is not controlled. Commercial trade in these species is permitted, but only if the country of origin issues an export permit. Species included in Appendix II include bears, parrots, spotted cats, orchids and carnivorous plants. This Appendix also includes species that are not themselves in danger of extinction, but which look very similar to another species that is endangered, as this helps customs officials to enforce the laws.

CITES has undoubtedly done a lot to reduce trade in endangered species, but it is not a perfect answer to species conservation. For example, banning legitimate trade in ivory has resulted in an increase in the price that can be obtained for smuggled ivory. This has provided an incentive to poachers of elephants, who – if they are prepared to break laws – can obtain a very high return for elephant tusks. People involved in the Campfire project (p. 84) would like to be able to sell the ivory obtained from elephants culled as part of their conservation programme. This would reduce the incentive for poaching and provide income that could be fed back into the project.

The pitcher plants, *Nepenthes*, are included in CITES Appendix II.

2 Explain why including non-endangered species in the CITES Appendix II may help customs officials.

KEY FACTS

- Species conservation focuses on the protection of individual species.

- Where possible, species should be conserved in their natural habitat.

- Captive breeding programmes can help to conserve species that are in danger of extinction in their natural environment.

- Such programmes attempt to maximise genetic diversity within the species by encouraging outbreeding (matings between unrelated animals or cross-pollination in plants).

- Where animals do not easily breed in captivity, techniques such as artificial insemination are used.

- If possible, a captive breeding programme should lead to reintroduction of the animal or plant to its natural environment.

- CITES is an international agreement that controls trade in endangered species or products made from them.

6.3 Nature conservation

Most conservation programmes go further than focusing on the conservation of individual species. Nature conservation entails maintaining a wide variety of habitats, within which many different species are able to live. One example of this type of conservation is the designation and management of Sites of Special Scientific Interest (SSSIs).

CASE STUDY

Wildmoor Heath Nature Reserve

This rare oblong-leaved sundew is found only in valley mire, like that shown opposite.

The reserve contains a wide range of habitats, including some that are very uncommon in this area and indeed in the UK. This is what makes the reserve a special area. Dry heath (above) supports gorse and heather.

Wildmoor Heath Nature Reserve is a 99 hectare site that lies between Crowthorne and Sandhurst, in Berkshire. It contains two SSSIs, and is owned partly by the Berkshire, Buckinghamshire and Oxfordshire Wildlife Trust (BBOWT) and partly by Bracknell Forest Borough Council (BFBC). These two organisations work together in managing the reserve.

One of the first tasks when managing such a reserve is to find out what is already there. Species lists have been made for the site, and decisions made about which of these species are to be 'priority species' when decisions are made about managing the reserve. Priority species include some for which there is concern on an international scale (e.g. Dartford warblers, nightjars and adders), some which appear to be safe in the world as a whole but for which there is national concern (e.g. silver studded blue butterflies and bog bush-crickets), and some for which there is regional concern (e.g. kingfishers and glow worms).

The list of priority species helps in deciding what is the best way to conserve them, and species diversity in general, within the reserve. A list of management principles has been drawn up, outlining what should be done in the reserve. For example, in some of the wetter areas, the community is dominated by a tussocky grass called *Molinia*. It is planned to manage the *Molinia*-dominated areas in such a way as to reduce the dominance of *Molinia* in favour of a more diverse community. This can be done by maintaining a high water table and putting cattle to graze on these areas.

As in many nature reserves, management plans must consider the need for public access without allowing it to have a deleterious effect. The reserve is sandwiched between two big population centres and many people use it for recreations such as dog walking, horse riding and bird watching. Visitor pressure is quite high, and there is a danger that disturbance from visitors could damage biodiversity within the reserve.

Free-running dogs are a particular concern, because they cause birds that nest close to the ground – which includes all of the priority bird species in the reserve – to abandon their nests. It is planned to make new paths in the less sensitive parts of the reserve, such as the woodland areas, and to stop people walking in the more sensitive areas, such as the open heath. However, it is very important that people should continue to feel welcome in the reserve, because it is they who are paying for it – either through taxes, lottery tickets or voluntary donations. Many people who live in the surrounding area volunteer to work in the reserve on particular projects.

1 Just to the east of the Wildmoor Heath reserve there are 580 hectares of woodland, containing some heathland and water-logged areas. Just to the west, there is another SSSI, containing bog habitats. The reserve is separated from these areas by patches of unprotected land. The groups managing Wildmoor Heath Nature Reserve would like to link up their reserve with these two areas. Suggest the possible benefits of this for conservation in the area.

Thanks to Richard Elston and the Berkshire, Buckinghamshire and Oxfordshire Wildlife Trust.

SSSIs

In England, Scotland and Wales, a number of SSSIs have been designated. These areas may be interesting because they contain unusual habitats, have very high biodiversity, or have interesting geological formations. SSSIs are often quite small. They include a wide variety of different habitats – for example heathland, woodland, meadows or wetlands. The sites are designated as SSSIs by government-funded organisations in each country – English Nature, Scottish Natural Heritage or the Countryside Council for Wales. There are currently nearly 6500 SSSIs in England, Scotland and Wales, and more sites are designated each year.

The main protection given to SSSIs is that any activity which might damage the site must be notified to the relevant designating organisation before it is undertaken. This can work well, but does not always do so, and many SSSIs are irreparably damaged each year. New legislation in 2001 has given greater protection to SSSIs.

KEY FACTS

■ Nature conservation aims to maintain a wide variety of habitats in an area.

■ SSSIs are areas that contain rare species, or types of habitat that are under threat, or have a high biodiversity. Their management aims to maintain a wide variety of habitats.

6.4 Biological conservation

Biological conservation aims to maintain biodiversity within habitats. This type of conservation tends to focus on areas where biodiversity is relatively high, and to manage these sites for the benefit of the wide range of species that live there.

Biodiversity action plans

In 1992, world leaders attended a conference in Rio de Janeiro in Brazil, to consider the sustainable use of the Earth's resources. The conference was known as the Earth Summit, and out of it grew a Convention on Biological Diversity. This convention was signed by 157 countries. Each country has committed itself to develop national strategies to protect its biodiversity.

In the UK, this resulted in a strategy that was published in 1994 by the Department of the Environment and entitled 'Biodiversity – the UK Action Plan'. This plan lists 59 objectives for conserving species and their habitats. It is being implemented by a range of organisations, including government-funded ones such as English Nature, and local wildlife trusts. Local Biodiversity Action Plans (BAPs) have been drawn up for all parts of the UK.

SSSIs can have a major role to play in supporting BAPs. Another type of site that helps to implement BAPs are National Nature Reserves, or NNRs. These areas were established to protect important areas of wildlife habitat, and are managed to maintain or increase biodiversity. They are administered by English Nature, Scottish Natural Heritage and the Countryside Council for Wales.

However, it is increasingly realised that it is not enough to focus conservation on a few patches of specially-designated land scattered throughout the country. More broadly-focused plans are being developed to help to maintain biodiversity in the countryside and also in urban environments. For example, the planting and maintenance of hedges can be encouraged. Hedges are ideal habitats for many species of plants and animals, and they can form corridors along which animals can travel between woods. Countryside Stewardship Schemes can give grants to farmers for leaving wide margins around the edges of arable fields, thus providing habitats for birds such as the grey partridge.

Many species cannot thrive unless they have a wide area of land to range over. When the conservation areas themselves cannot be made larger, it can help to establish **buffer zones** around them. These are areas in which farming and other activities are undertaken with sympathy for wildlife. This means that the edges of the 'proper' conservation area are protected from potentially damaging influences outside.

CASE STUDY   **Fragmentation of tropical rainforests**

International efforts are being made to attempt to conserve some of the world's increasingly endangered tropical rainforests. Tropical rainforests currently cover about 6% of the Earth's surface, yet they are thought to contain around half of the total number of species on Earth. Almost 75% of all known arthropods are found only in tropical rainforests. No-one is sure why biodiversity in these forests is so high, but it is probably at least partly due to the ideal conditions for plant growth that are found there. High rainfall and high temperatures provide an environment in which many different plant species have evolved and provide a wide range of niches for animals that interact with them.

Tropical rainforests are under considerable threat; it is estimated that at least 1% of these forests are being lost each year. Commercial logging companies cut down big areas each year to sell as timber. Forest is also cut down and burnt to produce new land for growing crops. This happens both on a small scale – for example, in slash-and-burn systems of agriculture, where families burn an area of forest and then grow crops on the land for a few years before moving on – and on a very large one, where forest is destroyed before huge stands of crops such as oil palms and coffee plantations are planted. Fires started locally may run out of control, especially in years when rainfall has been low. People also cut down trees to use as fuel.

Tropical rainforest is by no means the only type of habitat under grave threat, but the loss is particularly worrying because of the exceptionally high biodiversity. When forest is lost, so is the habitat for very high numbers of species. Many of these species may not yet have been discovered, especially those that live high in the canopy about which relatively little is known.

In many tropical countries, some areas of rainforest are protected, or at least are undamaged so far. However, these areas are often relatively small, and may be separated from each other by unforested areas. This situation is known as **fragmentation**, and it leads to a lowering of biodiversity. Small areas of forest are not capable of supporting such a high biodiversity as are large areas. Isolated populations of a particular species living in a forest fragment are much more likely to die out, than if they could freely intermix with other populations. And some species, particularly top carnivores, need very large areas in which to hunt.

Brazilian rainforest (bright green) with areas cleared for crops (yellow and brown).

Plants are affected by fragmentation as much as animals are. A study carried out in Brazil looked at more than 64 000 large trees over a period of 20 years. Some of them grew in continuous forest, while others grew in forest fragments ranging from 1 to 100 hectares in area. During this period, 6348 of the trees that were growing within 300 metres of the edge of the forest died; of those growing further than 300 metres from the edge, only 3523 died. The bar chart below shows the percentage difference in mortality of trees growing on the edges of patches of rainforest compared with trees growing well inside the forest.

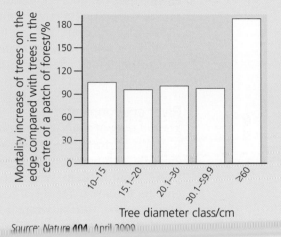
Source: Nature 404, April 2000

These findings, and the results of many other research programmes looking at the effects of deforestation and fragmentation on species diversity, provide a strong argument for making sure that any rainforest reserves are as large as possible. It is also very helpful if reserves in different parts of a country can be linked with corridors of protected forest so that animals can travel between them. For example, the charity Rainforest Concern is buying land to create a rainforest corridor between two large reserves in Ecuador. This corridor, the Choco-Andean Corridor, will have buffer zones on either side of it, in which the forest will not be completely protected, but where sustainable forms of income generation for the local population will be developed. These people, like most others who live near to rainforests, fully appreciate their value in both material and aesthetic terms. Some will be employed as rangers and guards.

1 Suggest why a population of animals living in a small, isolated fragment of rainforest is likely to have less genetic diversity than if it were in contact with other areas of the rainforest.

2 Describe the results shown in the bar chart, and suggest explanations for them.

6.5　Environmental conservation

Environmental conservation focuses on attempting to conserve the abiotic characteristics of ecosystems. This can help to ensure that habitats remain undamaged, and provide appropriate environments in which a wide range of organisms can live. In this section, we will concentrate on the ways in which the abiotic characteristics of rivers and other wetlands can be conserved.

River environments

Many kinds of river flow through the UK. Rivers that rise in, and flow through, upland areas tend to be fast-flowing and sometimes peaty. Their beds are swept clear of sediments, and are usually made up of rocks and boulders. In contrast, rivers flowing through the flat lands of eastern England are slow-moving, and tend to accumulate thick layers of muddy sediment in the river beds. The south of England has its chalk streams, fast-flowing and often famous for the excellent fishing that they provide.

The following abiotic factors have major effects on the species that live in a river, and their distribution and abundance.

pH of the water

This is largely determined by the soil and rocks over which the river flows. Rivers that flow through peaty moorlands generally contain water with a relatively low (acid) pH, while those that flow through limestone or chalk will have a higher (alkaline) pH.

Oxygen content of the water

Fast-flowing rivers tend to contain more dissolved oxygen than slow-flowing ones. This is especially true if the river is flowing over an uneven bed with large rocks in it, because the rocks break up the flow of the water and create turbulence. This increases the contact of the water surface with air, and therefore increases the rate at which oxygen from the air diffuses into the water. Oxygen content is also affected by organic pollutants that enter the river (Chapter 2). A polluted river tends to have a high BOD, which results in a low concentration of dissolved oxygen.

Rate of flow of the water

This is important because it affects the oxygen content, but it is also significant in its own right. Organisms that can live in slow-moving water may not be able to cope with fast-flowing, turbulent water – they would simply get swept away.

Composition of the river bed

Fast-flowing rivers tend to have rocky river beds, because the water sweeps away any finer material. Slow-flowing rivers are more likely to have beds made up of thick layers of mud, providing anchorage for aquatic plants.

Presence of pollutants

Some pollutants can lead to eutrophication (Chapter 2). Others have direct effects of their own – for example, pyrethroid chemicals used in sheep dips are very toxic to aquatic organisms. The effects of oil pollution are described in Chapter 2.

Clarity of the water

The clearer the water, the better light can penetrate it, and this affects the plants that grow in the river.

Temperature of the water

Water has a very high specific heat capacity, which means that it takes a lot of heat to make the temperature rise significantly. Even on a hot day, the water in a river feels cold. Most aquatic organisms are therefore not adapted to cope with big swings in temperature. However, some industries, for example power stations, produce warm water that they release into rivers. The raised temperature may in itself be harmful to some species, and warm water contains less dissolved oxygen than cold water.

3a Fish may be adapted to live in either cold or warm water (Fig. 1). Explain why the oxygen consumption of both fish species in Fig. 1 increases as temperature increases.

b Assuming that the cold-water species normally lives in water at 5 °C, while the warm-water species lives at 20 °C, suggest why the rate of oxygen consumption is greater for the cold-water species than the warm-water species, at all temperatures.

c Explain why having a very high oxygen consumption at high water temperatures is likely to be a problem for a fish.

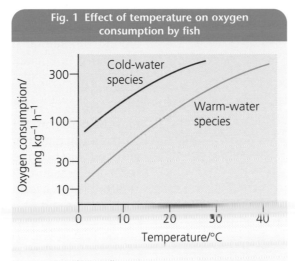

Fig. 1 Effect of temperature on oxygen consumption by fish

Source: Abel, Water Pollution Biology, Taylor & Francis, 1996

Some rivers have been canalised – the natural shape of the river bed has been completely reconstructed so the river becomes deeper and narrower. In some places, the river bed may be lined with concrete.

Human effects on the abiotic environment of rivers

There are few rivers in the UK, especially in England, that have not been altered in some way by human activity. To improve drainage, river beds may be dredged. Some rivers with winding paths have been straightened in order to make more use of the land around them.

These changes can have enormous effects on many abiotic factors associated with the river, and therefore on the organisms that live in it. For example, straightening or canalisation results in the loss of the natural variety of habitats that previously existed. In the natural river, some parts would have had fast water flow – for example, where the river narrows, or around the outside of a bend. Other parts would have had slow water flow – for example, where the river is especially wide, or on the inside of a bend. There may have been pools and waterfalls. Some parts of the unaltered bank may have been undercut by fast-flowing water, producing deep, steep and overhanging banks – these will not be present in the canalised river. Natural vegetation may have been removed from the river margins, or may no longer be able to grow there; this means loss of cover for semi-aquatic animals such as otters.

The taking of water for human use has also had enormous effects on some rivers. Water companies may take water directly from a river, or from other sources nearby that can eventually result in less water flowing in the river. This can result in a river completely drying up, especially in periods of drought. This happened to the River Kennet in southern England.

The volume of water that flows in a river may vary hugely at different times of year. In a particularly wet season, so much water may flow that the river bursts its banks, and water spreads over the surrounding land. Places where this happens regularly are known as **flood plains**. Flood plains are natural features, and they help to absorb the excess water. Without flood plains, the rate and magnitude of the rise in water volume in the river would be much greater and lead to flooding of other areas. Unfortunately, many homes have recently been built on flood plains (they are flat and easy to build on) and are at severe risk of flooding unless flood defences have been built, which means some other area is at risk.

Where a river's natural flood plain still survives, the land that regularly floods in autumn and winter may form **water meadows**. These grassy areas produce good grazing for farm animals when the water recedes in spring and summer, and also an excellent habitat for many different species of birds when they are flooded.

Conserving the abiotic environment of rivers and other wetlands

In recent years, the importance of trying to retain the natural environments of rivers has gradually been realised. Some rivers that were canalised are being restored to a more natural state. Major building projects are much less likely to take place on flood plains. The impact of water abstraction has been recognised, and moves are being made to reduce it.

In England, English Nature has designated nearly 30 rivers as SSSIs. This is about 2.5% of the total river length in England. These rivers have been chosen as the 'best of what is left', and are spread around the whole country (Fig. 2). Clearly, it is also important that the remaining 97.5% of river length is also treated with more care, and that, wherever possible, damaging changes inflicted in the past are reversed.

In 1971, an international agreement, the Conservation of Wetlands of International Importance, was signed at Ramsar in Iran by many countries, including the UK. So far, around 100 Ramsar sites have been designated in England, most of which are estuaries or reservoirs. Under the terms of the Ramsar Convention, if any part of a Ramsar site is damaged, then an equivalent habitat must be designated to take its place.

Unfortunately, during the 20th century, wet grassland has become an increasingly rare habitat in England. Between the 1930s and 1980s, it is estimated that it decreased by 40%, largely as a result of drainage for agriculture. In the Thames estuary alone, around 28 000 hectares of wet grassland has been lost. Of this, nearly 70% has been converted to arable land, while the rest is covered by industry and housing. The wet grassland that remains is very fragmented, and the Environment Agency and English Nature are working hard to conserve what we still have. The largest area of wet grassland in England is the Somerset Levels and Moors. Part of this area is already designated as Ramsar sites and SSSIs, and just under half is designated an Environmentally Sensitive Area (ESA). An ESA is a place where farmers are encouraged by grants to use the land in ways that are sympathetic to the natural environment.

Fig. 2 River SSSIs in England

Tweed
Coquet
Eden
Derwent
Cocker
Derwent
Malham-Arncliffe
Hull headwaters
Lathkill
Wensum
Blythe
Nar
Teme
Old Bedford
Wye
Lugg
Wye
Lambourn Kennet
Avon
Test
Beult
Moors
Itchen
Barle
Axe
De Lank
Frome
Lymington

Source: *Wildlife and Fresh Water*, English Nature, 1997

CASE STUDY ESA: Somerset Levels and Moors Natural Area

Source: *The Somerset Levels and Moors Natural Area*, English Nature, 1997

The Somerset Levels and Moors Natural Area is a large area of low-lying land in the south-west of England. It is bounded by the 10 m contour, and contains the most extensive area of lowland wet grassland and natural floodplain in England, which is of international importance. Eight major rivers flow through it, eventually emptying their waters into the Severn Estuary.

Eight thousand years ago, this area was an inlet of the sea. As the sea receded, the land became salt marsh and bog. The remains of dead plants did not decay completely in this wet anaerobic soil, but turned into peat. People have lived and farmed in this marshy area for thousands of years. A network of rivers plus constructed drains and ditches helps to drain the land in winter, and supply water in summer.

In 1987, the Ministry of Agriculture, Fisheries and Foods designated a large area of the Somerset Levels as an ESA. Increasing installation of drainage was causing a considerable change in the abiotic characteristics of the area. Farmers are now given the opportunity to join a scheme in which, in return for managing their land in ways that benefit the environment, they are compensated financially for the loss in productivity. The scheme was revised and renewed in 1997, and currently more than 65% of the grassland is protected from cultivation. The main management objectives are now to ensure that the water levels are not lowered any further and, in some areas, are raised to what they would have been many years ago. New dams,

sluices and culverts have been constructed to help with the control of water levels.

Farmers who opt to enter the ESA scheme must meet a number of criteria. These include:

- not introducing any new drainage to the land;
- maintaining all existing ditches;
- not spraying in or near ditches or drains;
- maintaining water levels at agreed heights during summer and winter;
- not ploughing or reseeding any grassland;
- only applying agreed levels of inorganic fertilisers – or in some cases not using any at all;
- not adding lime to the soil, which would reduce its natural acidity;
- following agreed guidelines on the grazing of cattle and sheep;
- cutting grass only for hay (not silage).

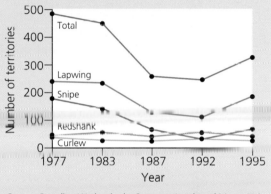

Source: *Breeding Waders in the Somerset Levels and Moors ESA*, RSPB/MAFF/EA/EN leaflet, (undated)

Water-level controls in the Somerset Levels are having a very beneficial effect on wildlife. For example, winter flooding benefits waders, and provides suitable areas in which they can nest in spring. The graph above shows changes in the number of breeding territories of five species of wading bird on eleven sites in the area (note that the area was designated an ESA in 1987).

1 Cutting grass for hay is normally done once a year, in June. Cutting grass for silage is normally done much earlier in the year than this, and usually second or even third cuts are made later on. Suggest why farmers in the ESA scheme are asked only to cut grass for hay, and not for silage.

Thanks to Stephen Parker and the English Nature Somerset Team.

Global conservation

Global conservation is conservation on a world scale. It involves the composition of the atmosphere and oceans, and international attempts to address problems such as the production of acid rain (Chapter 2), the damage that has been done to ozone levels in the upper atmosphere, and the emission of greenhouse gases. In this section, we will concentrate on greenhouse gases and high-level ozone, and consider our efforts to conserve the quality of our atmosphere.

Greenhouse gases and global warming

The Earth is kept warm because of radiation from the Sun (Fig. 3). A high proportion of this radiation has a short wavelength, and passes through the atmosphere to the ground. Here, some of it is re-emitted as radiation with a longer wavelength. This long wavelength radiation warms the atmosphere.

If we had no so-called 'greenhouse gases' in our atmosphere, then the long wavelength radiation would simply pass back out into space. The Earth would be much cooler than it is today – so cold, in fact, that there would be no liquid water. As it is, a small percentage of the atmosphere – between 0.03 and 0.04% – is carbon dioxide. This gas, along with water vapour, methane, nitrogen oxides and chlorofluorocarbons (CFCs) absorb much of

the long wavelength radiation and stop it from escaping into space. This is known as the **greenhouse effect**, because the gases behave rather like the glass in a greenhouse.

The greenhouse effect is a natural phenomenon, and without it there would be no humans living on Earth. However, the quantities of all the greenhouse gases have recently been steadily increasing. Moreover, the mean global temperature is also increasing (Fig. 4). This is called **global warming**, and is a matter of great importance for ourselves and all life on Earth.

There have been numerous occasions in the past when atmospheric carbon dioxide concentrations and mean global temperatures have fluctuated widely, The two often seem to go hand in hand, providing circumstantial evidence that one is causing the other. Carbon dioxide levels can increase for many reasons, for example a spate of volcanic eruptions. However, many people believe that the current rise (Fig. 3 inset) is caused by large-scale burning of fossil fuels.

No-one wants global warming to happen; it is likely to cause a multitude of major changes to climate in different parts of the world, though exactly what these will be is impossible to predict. Probably, some areas that currently have plenty of rainfall will become drier. Sea levels are likely to rise as ice caps melt, putting low-lying land such as Bangladesh and some islands in the Caribbean, Pacific Ocean and Indian Ocean at great risk of being at least partly submerged.

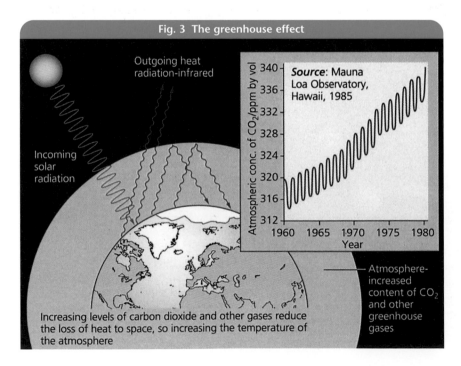

Fig. 3 The greenhouse effect

Outgoing heat radiation-infrared

Incoming solar radiation

Source: Mauna Loa Observatory, Hawaii, 1985

Atmospheric conc. of CO_2/ppm by vol

Year

Atmosphere-increased content of CO_2 and other greenhouse gases

Increasing levels of carbon dioxide and other gases reduce the loss of heat to space, so increasing the temperature of the atmosphere

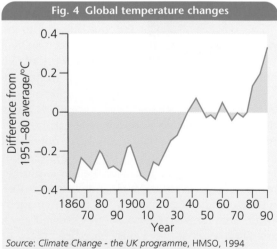

Fig. 4 Global temperature changes

Difference from 1951–80 average/°C

Year

Source: Climate Change - the UK programme, HMSO, 1994

Weather patterns may become more extreme, with a greater incidence of flooding or very high winds.

4 Suggest why the level of carbon dioxide shown in Fig. 3 (inset) shows regular annual variations.

There have therefore been several attempts to arrive at international agreements with the aim of reducing emissions of carbon dioxide and methane. After the 1992 international summit in Rio de Janeiro (p. 90), the UK government undertook to reduce carbon dioxide emissions to the level they were at in 1990. Methane emissions were to be reduced from the 1990 level by 10%, nitrous oxide by 75%, and CFC emissions would be halted completely. For carbon dioxide, this was to be done through reductions in energy use and, hence, reduction in the burning of fossil fuels. In the UK, most methane emissions are from the decay of rubbish in land-fill sites; it was proposed that these could be reduced by using this methane for energy generation. This, of course, would change the methane into carbon dioxide, but as methane is a much more effective greenhouse gas than carbon dioxide, this is still an improvement.

Significant success has been achieved by the UK and many other countries in achieving the targets they set after the Rio convention. However, we still have a long way to go if we are to halt global warming. An international convention held in Kyoto, Japan, in 2000 had still failed to reach agreement by 2001. A key sticking point was

the idea that countries could gain 'carbon dioxide credits' by not cutting down forests. The argument here is that photosynthesis by the trees helps to absorb carbon dioxide from the atmosphere. This proposition was strongly fought for by the USA, which is by far the largest producer of carbon dioxide (Fig. 5). Another problem is the idea that developing countries, which do not emit much carbon dioxide, could 'sell' their allowed carbon dioxide emissions to other countries, which would then be allowed to emit more carbon dioxide.

Unfortunately, we still do not understand enough about the processes that affect carbon dioxide in the atmosphere. Carbon dioxide concentrations have shown wide fluctuations over long periods of time, and we are not sure what caused them. We are not even able to state with scientific certainty that leaving a certain area of forest undamaged could make up for a particular amount of carbon dioxide emissions. These uncertainties have made it easier for countries such as the USA to resist international pressure for them to reduce their carbon dioxide emissions.

CFCs and the high-level ozone layer

We have had much more success in dealing with the damage to the ozone layer. This shows that it is possible for countries to work together to halt – even reverse – damage that we have done to the world environment in the past.

Ozone is a gas with the formula O_3. At ground level, it is produced from pollutant gases such as nitrogen dioxide (which can be

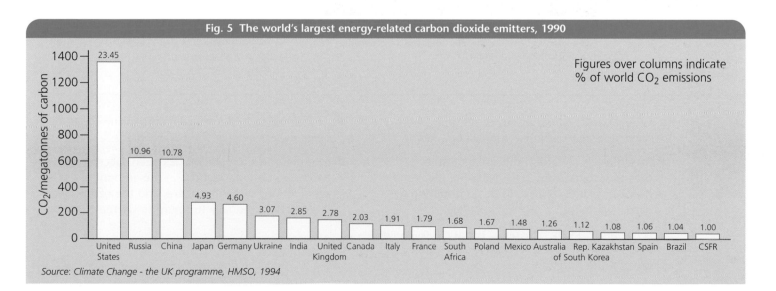

Fig. 5 The world's largest energy-related carbon dioxide emitters, 1990

Figures over columns indicate % of world CO_2 emissions

Source: Climate Change - the UK programme, HMSO, 1994

emitted from vehicle exhausts) reacting with sunlight. Here it is harmful, adversely affecting plant growth and the respiratory systems of animals, including humans. However, high in the Earth's atmosphere, about 20–35 km above the surface, there is a layer in which relatively large amounts of ozone are found. Ozone forms in this region because ultraviolet rays from the sun cause oxygen molecules to split and then recombine:

$$O_2 \rightarrow O + O$$
$$O_2 + O \rightarrow O_3$$

These reactions also happen in reverse. In the past, the forward and reverse reactions have taken place at about the same rate, so that the total amount of ozone in the high atmosphere tended to remain roughly constant.

The ozone layer is of great importance to all living things on Earth, because it absorbs a high proportion of the ultraviolet light from

the sun. Ultraviolet light can increase the risk of skin cancers, or melanomas. It can also cause cataracts to develop, and appears to have harmful effects on the growth of many types of plant.

5 Explain how ultraviolet radiation increases the chances of melanomas.

It was realised that loss of high-level ozone was caused by the release of CFCs into the atmosphere. (Do not confuse the role of CFCs here with their role as greenhouse gases.) CFCs were widely used as aerosol propellants and as coolants in refrigerators. No-one thought that they might have any harmful effects, because they are extremely unreactive.

However, we now know that their unreactivity is one of the major factors that contributes to their damaging effects in the high atmosphere. CFCs released at ground level slowly move throughout the atmosphere, eventually reaching the ozone layer. They remain unchanged throughout this time, lasting as much as 100 years without breaking down. However, when they reach the ozone layer, the chlorine atoms that they contain begin to react with ozone molecules, breaking them down into oxygen.

Most developed countries have now completely phased out the use of CFCs. Alternatives have been developed that do not – so far as we know – have such harmful effects. And it looks very much as though the problem is close to being solved. But it is going to take a while before the ozone layer is back to normal, because we cannot remove the CFCs that are already there. Still, this does look like a success story, and gives encouragement that it *is* possible for international action to be taken to reverse damage done to our environment.

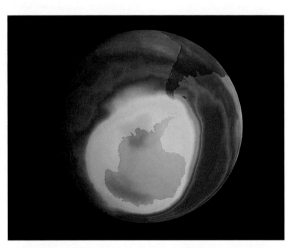

In this false-colour satellite image taken in 2000, the damage to the ozone layer can be seen as the yellow-green area under which Antartica is visible (dark green).

Species	Food	Typical body mass/g	Percentage of woods of each size inhabited by named species				
			0.001–0.01 ha	0.01–0.1 ha	0.1–1 ha	1–10 ha	10–100 ha
Blackbird	Wide range of insect and plant food	90	13	34	63	72	91
House sparrow	Weed and grass seeds	30	9	21	44	35	22
Great tit	Insects and nuts	20	0	3	12	16	73
Tree creeper	Insects	10	0	0	2	8	25
Great spotted woodpecker	Insects	130	0	0	0	1	26

1 The table shows the percentage of woods of different sizes which were inhabited by different bird species.

a Describe the relationship between the size of a wood and the diversity of the birds that it contains. (1)

b Use the data in the table to explain:
   i) the different distribution of tree creepers and great spotted woodpeckers; (1)
   ii) why very small woods are inhabited by house sparrows and blackbirds but not by great tits and tree creepers. (2)

c It has been suggested that planting trees on farmland would help conserve woodland birds. Use the information in this table to suggest advice that you could give to farmers who wanted to conserve woodland birds on their land

Explain your answer. (2)

BY0 March 99

2 Read the following passage.

1 The 400 000 hectares of bleak open moorland in the far north of Scotland constitute one of the finest 'blanket bogs' in the world. Although it supports relatively few species, this outstanding
5 ecosystem is a wonderful reservoir of wildlife more usually associated with the Arctic tundra. In the fragile peat grow highly specialised plants that are adapted to survive in the cold, wet, acidic conditions. Over 30 species of sphagnum
10 moss live there, each occupying its own niche within the bog. Other characteristic plants are the sundews, which are insectivorous. They overcome the shortage of nutrients such as nitrates by digesting small insects that are
15 trapped by long sticky hairs on the leaves. The bog is also an important breeding ground for

several species of bird, which make use of the vast numbers of insects and other invertebrates that proliferate in early summer. For instance,
20 about 70% of Britain's population of greenshanks breed here, before migrating to the coasts further south for the winter.
   However, this fragile ecosystem is threatened by extensive afforestation with conifers. Patches
25 of the forest already dot the landscape. Drainage work for each patch affects a much wider area than is to be planted, by lowering the water table and thus altering the habitat for the mosses. Predators such as foxes live in the forest,
30 and few birds nest within a kilometre of a forest patch. Patches of forest are, therefore, much more damaging than they might seem. The rate of growth of trees in this harsh habitat is slow, with many casualties due to fierce gales. Without
35 the tax incentives made available by the government, afforestation in this area might well not be economic.

a i) Explain what is meant by 'niche' (line 10). (1)
   ii) Explain how drainage work could cause the elimination of some species of moss. (1)

b Suggest why the ecosystem supports 'relatively few species' (line 4). (2)

c Suggest the advantage to the greenshank of migrating from its breeding grounds to the coast (lines 19–22). (1)

d Sundew plants are able to digest insects trapped on their leaves. Explain how this is of benefit to the sundews in this environment. (3)

e Evaluate the case for growing trees in this habitat. (4)

BY05 March 00

Answers to questions

Answers to in-text questions and questions in case-study boxes are given below. Answers to examination questions are not included.

Chapter 1

1 It is much quicker and easier to make decisions when using the ACFOR scale. However, this gives less precise data than if you estimated percentage cover.

2 Total number in population =
$$\frac{54 \times 63}{18} = 189$$

3

a Your table should look like Table 1.

Table 1 Data from 200 randomly placed point quadrats in field			
Species	***n***	***n*–1**	***n*(*n*–1)**
Grass	185	184	34040
Thistles	28	27	756
Stinging nettles	35	34	1190
Moss	2	1	2
Total (*N*) = 250			
Total *n*(*n*–1) = 35988			

b $D = \dfrac{250 \times 249}{35988} = 1.73$

c The needle has hit more than one plant in many of the point quadrat samples.

d The species diversity in the field is much less that that in the lawn. We can only guess the reasons for this. Some possibilities would be:
- the sheep graze selectively in the field – perhaps they do not eat thistles or nettles, but have grazed so heavily on other plants that they cannot grow;
- perhaps the field has been sprayed with a selective weedkiller, whereas no spray has been used on the lawn;
- perhaps the soil in the field and lawn differ in their mineral content.
  You can probably think of other possible explanations.

e The same method has been used in both places, and the same total number of point quadrat samples were used in each, so they are comparable. However, no attempt was made to differentiate between grass species in the field. If there were two or more different species of grass present, this would increase the calculated value for species diversity.

Case study boxes
Red grouse populations

1

a The two grouse populations treated with the worm-killing drug in 1989 (represented by curves b and c) did not crash, while the untreated one (curve a) did. In 1993, the two untreated populations (curves a and b) did crash, while the population which was treated with the drug (curve c) did not.

b In those populations that were treated with the drug, the numbers did still drop a little in the years when a crash was expected. This can be seen in curve (b) in 1989, and in curve (c) in both 1989 and 1993.

Chapter 2

1

a The minimal dissolved oxygen concentration occurs where there is maximum activity of aerobic bacteria. At the point of discharge, the microbial population has not reached its maximum level. An additional factor may be that the products of microbial breakdown lead to eutrophication – excess growth of algae and plants – and the decay of these further stimulates microbial activity and, therefore, oxygen depletion.

b Once the effluent has been broken down, there is much less organic material for microorganisms to feed on and, therefore, fewer microorganisms to reduce the oxygen concentration. The minerals that are released as a result of the action of the bacteria on the effluent stimulate the growth of plants and algae which, provided they are not in excess, release oxygen into the water as they photosynthise. A flowing river also absorbs oxygen from the air, especially if the surface is turbulent.

2

a You want to know the oxygen concentration of the *water*, not the air. Oxygen in an air bubble may dissolve in the water and alter the results.

b In the light, any photosynthetic organisms in the water would release oxygen, which would confuse the results.

3 The reason is probably interspecific competition. These organisms are probably unable to compete successfully with species that can live in well-oxygenated water but cannot live in poorly oxygenated water.

4

a Site 1 = 5.16; Site 2 = 2.49

b Site 1 has a much higher diversity index than Site 2, showing that Site 1 is better oxygenated, almost certainly because it is less polluted with organic effluent or nitrates than Site 2.

5 The stone loach is much more tolerant of cadmium than the trout. The trout can tolerate almost double the dose of zinc. Both are susceptible to relatively low doses of copper, although it takes longer to have an effect in the trout.

6

a Shrimp and limpet.

b Chironomid fly and simulid fly.

Case study boxes
Mercury pollution in Minamata Bay

1

a Cell membranes, including the cell surface membrane, are made from a bilayer of phospholipids. So, substances that can dissolve in lipids are able to diffuse readily through membranes and into living cells.

b The methyl mercury tended to remain in the enclosed bay, rather than spread out into the rest of the sea. If it had been able to spread more quickly and widely, then it would have been diluted in much larger volumes of sea water. It would probably not have built up in such high concentrations in living organisms, and the local human population would not have acquired so much of it in the seafood that they ate.

c The mercury compounds within living organisms are not broken down, but bioaccumulate.

The *Amoco Cadiz* oil spill

1

a Detergent enables oil to disperse in water, so it can damage lipids on the surface of, or within, living organisms. Detergents may be just as toxic, or even more so, to living organisms as the oil itself.

b Gases and carbon particles will be released into the air, which may cause different pollution problems. It is also possible that toxic products from the burning will dissolve in the sea water, where they may further harm living organisms.

Chapter 3

1 The black forms absorb heat more quickly, and so their body temperature tends to be higher than that of individuals with zig-zag patterning. As summers are short and cool, this means that the black snakes can grow faster than the zig-zag ones.

2 As the air in the burrow remains relatively humid, the difference in concentration between this air and the air in the animal's lungs is relatively small. This reduces the diffusion gradient for water vapour, so less is lost from the lungs. Moreover, the relatively low temperature in the burrow reduces the tendency of liquid water to evaporate from the lungs, and also reduces diffusion rates.

3

a Animals that live in habitats where water is in short supply excrete a much more concentrated urine than those that live in habitats with plentiful water. Aquatic animals seem to produce the least concentrated urine of all.

b It would be expected that animals living in dry habitats would have thick medullas, while those living in habitats with ample water would have thin medullas.

4 Average temperature and light intensity are highest in Texas, and gradually decrease as you travel further north. C_4 plants have the

greatest advantage over C_3 plants in areas of high temperature and high light intensity, and so this is where they are most common.

Case study boxes

Halophytes

1 Increasing human populations mean that more and more land is needed for growing crops. In many countries where rainfall is low, there is little fresh water available for irrigation. Irrigation with salty water quickly results in a build up of salts in the soil. It would be very useful to be able to grow crops that can tolerate high salt levels in the soil, or in the water that is used for irrigation.

How do birds know when and where to migrate?

1 Hand-raised birds were used to avoid the possibility of them learning behaviour patterns from the parent birds.

2 The birds are pre-programmed to fly in a particular direction. The swallows inherit a genetic mechanism that determines which way they orient themselves at the beginning of their migratory flight.

Chapter 4

1

a Abiotic factors are: intensity and duration of light; availability of water, temperature, and inorganic ions; carbon dioxide concentration. The others are **biotic** factors.

b Tropical forest: a high density of trees and other tropical plants, warm temperatures throughout the year extending the growing season, no shortage of soil nutrients or water, all contribute to the high productivity. Intensive agriculture: a high density planting of crops during the growing season, application of nitrogenous fertilisers and possibly irrigation, all contribute to the high productivity.

c Extreme desert and desert scrub: lack of water (and, therefore, lack of plants) and lack of soil nutrients reduce productivity.

2 NPP = GPP − respiration
= 8732 − 2045
= 6687 kg of glucose per 0.5 hectare per 100 days
You could double these figures, so that the values you calculate are for one hectare rather than 0.5 hectare.

3 150 kg ha^{-1}, or slightly less. This concentration results in maximum grain yield. Any less will result in reduced grain yield. Any more will also result in less grain yield and extra expense.

4 At low P, nitrogen is the limiting factor up to about 100 kg ha^{-1}. After that, phosphorus is limiting. At high P, nitrogen limits root yield up to about 100 mg ha^{-1}. After that, there is a slight decrease which may be due to the lack of some other ion such as potassium.

5 b Yield increases with increased application of N fertiliser but the increase is less at high N fertiliser levels.

c 13.6, 8.6, 6.27, 54.8 respectively.

d Yes.

e 100 kg ha^{-1} is the most economical. After this, increasing fertiliser application does not result in similar increases in yield.

6

a The fertiliser applications for spring barley are much lower when it is grown after roots compared with when it is grown after cereals. The root crop must use up less nutrients than cereals.

b Winter wheat requires more nitrogen, while sugar beet requires more phosphorus and much more potassium.

c Excess nutrients may leach out of the soil, and so be wasted. They could cause eutrophication in rivers and streams. Yields will be reduced.

7

a Light intensity.

b Either some other factor, such as carbon dioxide, is limiting the rate of photosynthesis, or the increased temperature is decreasing the activity of enzymes involved in photosynthesis.

8 To evaluate the effects of carbon dioxide as a limiting factor, you must compare increases in carbon dioxide when all other factors (light intensity and temperature) are constant. At a chosen light intensity and at 15 °C, an increase in carbon dioxide from 0.03% to 0.13% brings about a large increase in photosynthetic rate. At the same light intensity but at 25 °C, an increase in carbon dioxide from 0.03% to 0.13% brings about an even greater increase in the rate.

9 Advantages include: reapplication of the insecticide is needed less often; it may be cheaper since less insecticide is used; labour costs are reduced. Disadvantages include: the insecticide is more likely to remain on crops and be ingested by humans or other animals, with possible toxic effects; it could affect useful insects; it is more likely to accumulate in food chains; there is increased chance of resistance developing in pest populations as a result of natural selection.

10
a 0.04 kg ha^{-1}; 0.52 kg ha^{-1}
b There is an increasing likelihood of reaching toxic or lethal doses for non-target species. The rate of bioaccumulation will also increase, with a greater chance of effects on organisms higher up the food chain.

11 The fluctuation is a result of some kind of density-dependent factor, as described in Chapter 1. This could be interaction between predator and prey, including the control agent.

Case study boxes
Biological control: success stories

1 The biological control agent cannot disperse, and its population can be maintained at a high enough level to control the pest population. There is less chance of the agent affecting natural ecosystems, or being affected by them. Environmental conditions are likely to be kept at a favourable level for the activity and reproduction of the control agent.

Farming in Britain since the mid 20th century

1 More fossil fuels are used in fertiliser production, transport and application adding to the problems of increasing carbon dioxide concentrations and

their possible effects on global warming. High nitrate concentration allows some plants to grow vigorously, increasing competition with smaller species and so decreasing species diversity. Leaching of nitrates into waterways can cause eutrophication, again reducing species diversity.

Chapter 5

1 At X, the maximum sustainable yield is being taken. This means that $(C + M) = (A + G)$ – or, in other words, the biomass of fish being taken equals the natural increase in biomass in the population. Above X, the fishing effort is taking more fish than are naturally replaced. $(C + M)$ is greater than $(A + G)$, so the fish population decreases. This means that smaller catches will result.

2 The percentage reduction in each quota is given in Table 2.

Table 2 Percentage reductions in UK fishing quotas in the North Sea between 2000 and 2001	
Species	Percentage reduction
Haddock	21
Cod	45
Whiting	32
Plaice	20
Hake	41

This suggests the reduction in the cod quota *may* have the greatest impact. It is the greatest percentage reduction (45%), and the cod fishery is the second largest in the list. However, as fishermen were not able to reach their quotas in 1999, the *actual* reduction in fish caught will not be as great as 45% . The reduction in the quota for hake is almost as great (41%) but the hake fishery is very small compared with the cod fishery, so this is unlikely to have a very significant effect.

Without knowing the relative prices of each species of fish, it is not really possible to predict the severity of these cuts.

3
a The minimum mesh sizes have mostly been increased. The number of different mesh sizes allowable in

various areas in the north-east Atlantic has been reduced from six to two.
b Having only two allowed mesh sizes, each in its own area, makes it easier for fishermen to understand the rules, and for inspectors to enforce them.
c The increase in minimum mesh sizes should reduce the number of small fish caught as more can escape through the larger holes.

4 The fish that are farmed in any quantity in the UK (salmon and trout) are not species that are caught (at least, not in any significant numbers) by sea fishermen.

Case study boxes
Potential environmental effects of the salmon farming industry

1 Filter-feeding shellfish help to remove suspended particles of waste food or faeces, so reducing the possibility of eutrophication. Algae absorb and use dissolved inorganic ions, such as nitrate or ammonium, that could otherwise also result in eutrophication. The algae release oxygen into the water as they photosynthesise, helping the water to remain well oxygenated.

Chapter 6

1 Mammalian embryos develop inside the mother. The time this takes – gestation time – is time during which she is unable to conceive any more offspring. If, however, the fertilised eggs from a female of the endangered species are allowed to develop in the uterus of a female of another species, then the endangered female is free to produce more eggs. In effect, lots of uteruses can be used to grow her embryos all at once, whereas her own might only be able to grow one at a time.

2 Some species are not easy to identify, and customs officials are very unlikely to be expert botanists or zoologists. If similar species to endangered ones are also banned, then it is easier for customs officials to stop the export or import of the endangered species.

3
a Fish are ectothermic animals – that is, their body temperature depends on the temperature of their environment.

As water temperature rises, so does body temperature. Therefore, the rate of metabolic reactions, including respiration, also increases.

b The cold water species is adapted to live at 5 °C, when its oxygen consumption is about 100 mg kg^{-1} h^{-1}. The warm species is adapted to live at 20 °C, and at this temperature its oxygen consumption is also around 100 mg kg^{-1} h^{-1}. The cold-water graph is, therefore, always higher than the warm-water one at the same temperature.

c As temperature rises, so does the concentration of dissolved oxygen. So, while the fish's requirement for oxygen is increasing, the availability of oxygen is decreasing.

4 During summer, when light intensity is relatively high and days are long, more photosynthesis takes place and removes more carbon dioxide from the atmosphere. So, levels drop each summer and rise each winter.

5 Ultraviolet radiation damages DNA, and therefore can cause mutations. Some of these may be in genes that control whether or not cells divide, and if this control is lost then cancer may result.

Case study boxes
The Millennium Seed Bank and the St Helena boxwood

1 Research needs to be done to find out what conditions this species needs for survival – for example, soil type, water availability and so on. It would also be useful to know other information about it, such as how the flowers are pollinated, how the seeds are dispersed, and what conditions the seeds require for germination. Once this is known, then St Helena can be searched to find suitable sites where the boxwood would be expected to be able to survive. These sites will need protection, perhaps by fencing, to ensure that grazing or human disturbance do not threaten the newly introduced plants.

The scimitar-horned oryx

1

a The more the local people support the project, the more likely it is to succeed. There is less chance that there will be poaching of the introduced oryx, and less likelihood that land taken over for the reserve will be reclaimed by local people for farming or other purposes.

b Local people need to be involved in the project as much as possible, for example by being employed as wardens on the reserves. If possible, other ways of ensuring that money goes into the local economy as a result of the project should be found, for example by encouraging tourists to visit the reserves.

Wildmoor Heath Nature Reserve

1 Such a link up would give opportunity for animals to move between the different areas, helping genes to flow between populations that may be otherwise isolated from one another. This would maintain or increase genetic diversity. There would be similar benefits for plant species, as cross-pollination becomes more likely, and seed dispersal could occur more easily into new areas. There is less likelihood of a small, isolated population of animals or plants becoming extinct.

Fragmentation of tropical rainforests

1 It is likely that the sum total of the different alleles in the isolated population will be less than that for all the animals of that species. Over time, as inbreeding occurs, more and more alleles are likely to be lost.

2 The results show that, for all sizes of trees, mortality was higher on the edge of the forest than in the centre. This effect is greatest for the largest trees. There are several possible reasons for this. Trees on forest edges are more exposed to high winds than in the forest interior, and this is likely to cause more damage to very tall trees than to smaller ones. They get more sunlight, and this may mean that they are more likely to have climbers such as lianas (woody climbing plants) growing up them, which can reduce their life-span. And they are more exposed to drying air than are trees inside the very humid deep forest.

Environmental conservation in the Somerset Levels and Moors Natural Area

1 Cutting in June allows flowering plants that grow with the grass to flower and set seed, so ensuring that the biodiversity of the grassland does not decrease. Cutting earlier, and then again later in the year, does not allow this to happen, and some species of plants are likely to be lost from the grassland.

Glossary

abiotic factors
Factors resulting from non-living parts of an ecosystem.

abundance scale
A scale such as the ACFOR scale, in which a species is recorded as being Abundant, Common, Frequent, Occasional or Rare.

acid rain
Precipitation with a pH lower than 5.6.

antagonism
The interaction between two factors where the effect of one at least partly cancels out the effect of the other.

aquaculture
Farming aquatic organisms, such as fish and shellfish.

artificial fertiliser
A fertiliser made from inorganic components, such as ammonium nitrate.

belt transect
A type of transect in which sampling takes place in quadrats placed with one side on the line defined by the transect.

bioaccumulation
The increase in the concentration of a substance in the bodies of animals as it passes along a food chain.

biochemical oxygen demand (BOD)
The rate at which oxygen is used up in an aquatic environment; a high BOD indicates a high level of pollution.

biological conservation
Conservation that attempts to maintain species diversity within a habitat.

biological control
The use of a natural predator or parasite to reduce the population size of a pest species.

biomass
The mass of biological material present in, for example, a habitat.

biotic factors
Factors resulting from living parts of an ecosystem.

biotic index
A number that is assigned to a particular species indicating its ability to survive in water of low oxygen concentration. Species with a high biotic index can only survive where oxygen levels are high; those with a low biotic index can survive in poorly oxygenated water.

broad-spectrum herbicide
A broad-spectrum herbicide is one that harms many different plants, not just the targeted plant. Also called a non-selective herbicide.

buffer zones
Areas surrounding conservation areas in which human activities are controlled to some extent, but not as fully as within the conservation area itself.

bundle sheath cells
Cells in the leaves of C_4 plants in which rubisco is kept away from direct contact with air.

by-catch
Fish that are caught unintentionally along with the targeted fish; that is fish of the wrong species, or that are too small.

C_3 plants
Plants in which the first product of photosynthesis is a 3-carbon sugar.

C_4 plants
Plants in which the first product of photosynthesis is a 4-carbon sugar; many C_4 plants grow in the tropics.

captive breeding
Breeding animals, usually from a species that is endangered in the wild, in controlled conditions, with the aim of increasing the size and genetic diversity of the population.

carrying capacity
The maximum population size that can be sustainably maintained in a habitat.

CITES
The Convention on International Trade in Endangered Species of Wild Fauna and Flora, which regulates the movement of endangered species, or products obtained from them, between countries.

climax community
The final community that exists at the end of succession.

closed systems
A closed system of aquaculture grows fish in artificial conditions, for example in cages in a sea loch, or inside buildings.

competition
Interaction between two or more organisms where each needs the same resource, which is in short supply.

contact herbicide
A herbicide that is absorbed through the leaf surface of a plant, and is not transported inside the plant.

cover trap
A piece of wood or stone under which invertebrates may accumulate and can be captured.

crop rotation
Growing different crops on a piece of land in successive years.

crude oil
Oil as it is first obtained from the ground, before it has been separated into its individual components.

demersal fish
Fish that live on or near the sea bed.

density-dependent factors
Factors whose intensity of action increases as population size increases, and decreases as population size decreases.

density-independent factors
Factors whose intensity of action is not directly related to the size (density) of a population.

diversity
See species diversity.

diversity index
A formula for calculating species diversity, e.g. Simpson's Diversity Index, Margalef Index.

ecological factors
Any features of the environment, either living or non-living, that affect the distribution or abundance of a species.

ectothermic
An ectothermic organism relies on heat sources outside its body, but can often partially regulate its body temperature by behavioural means.

edaphic factors
Factors resulting from the type and structure of the soil.

endogenous
Endogenous control is the result of events within an organism's body, not affected by external factors such as change in daylength.

endothermic
An endothermic organism regulates its body temperature by generating heat by metabolic reactions (especially respiration) inside its body.

environmental conservation
Conservation that attempts to maintain the abiotic factors in a particular ecosystem.

eutrophication
The result of an increase in nutrients in an aquatic system, when populations of aerobic bacteria increase and oxygen levels drop.

extensive farming
Extensive farming uses relatively large areas of land and low inputs (fertilisers, pesticides, etc.) to produce a crop or to rear animals.

flood plains
Areas of low-lying land that are naturally flooded when water levels in rivers and streams rise.

fragmentation
The break-up of a habitat into several small fragments; it can cause large reductions in species diversity.

frame quadrat
A square that defines the area within which data are collected.

fungicide
A substance that kills fungi.

gene banks
Stores of many individuals of a species with as wide a range of genotypes as possible; for example, plants may be stored as seeds, animals as adult individuals or as frozen sperm and eggs.

genetic diversity
The range of different alleles found in a population.

global conservation
Conservation on a worldwide scale, involving cooperation between many countries.

global warming
An increase in the average global temperatures on Earth, which appears to be resulting from an increase in the concentration of carbon dioxide in the atmosphere.

greenhouse effect
The maintenance of relatively warm temperatures on Earth, because of the presence of carbon dioxide and other 'greenhouse gases' in the atmosphere; it is a natural effect without which the Earth would be too cold to support life.

halophytes
Plants that are adapted for survival in places where the water has a high concentration of dissolved salts, such as in estuaries.

herbicide
A substance that kills weeds.

inbreeding
Breeding between closely-related individuals; it tends to reduce genetic diversity.

indicator species
Species whose distribution is strongly correlated with the degree of pollution, and whose presence or absence can, therefore, be used as a measure of pollution.

insecticide
A substance that kills insects.

integrated pest management (IPM)
The use of both chemical methods and biological control in such a way that they act together to keep pests or weeds under control.

intensive farming
Intensive farming uses relatively small areas of land and high inputs (fertilisers, pesticides, etc.) to maximise the yield from a crop or from animals.

interrupted belt transect
A type of transect in which sampling takes place in quadrats placed at intervals along the line defined by the transect.

interspecific competition
Competition between members of different species.

intraspecific competition
Competition between members of the same species.

kick sampling
Catching aquatic invertebrates by standing in running water and disturbing the bottom with a foot, while holding a net downstream.

kinesis
A response to a stimulus in which an animal's rate of movement, or frequency of turning, is affected by the external conditions.

law of diminishing returns
The situation in which increasing applications of fertiliser eventually fail to give increasing crop yields.

LC_{50}
The concentration of a substance that kills 50% of a population; LC stands for lethal concentration.

LD_{50}
The amount of a substance that kills 50% of a population; LD stands for lethal dose.

leaf area index (LAI)
The percentage of the ground surface that is covered by leaves.

legumes
Plants such as peas, beans, alfalfa and clover, which have nitrogen-fixing bacteria in their root nodules.

limiting factor
The factor that is in shortest supply and is limiting the rate of a process such as photosynthesis.

Lincoln Index
The formula for calculating population size when using the mark–release–recapture technique: total number in population = number in 1st sample × number in 2nd sample ÷ number of marked animals in 2nd sample.

line transect
A type of transect in which sampling takes place at every point along the line.

Longworth trap
A trap that is baited with food to attract and catch small mammals.

Margalef Index
A formula for calculating species diversity.

mark–release–recapture
A sampling technique in which a sample of organisms is marked and released back into its habitat; a second

sample is then taken and can be used to calculate the overall population size using the Lincoln Index.

maximum sustainable yield
The maximum biomass of fish that can be taken from a population without causing any long-term decrease in the size of that population.

microclimate
The abiotic factors in a particular small area of a habitat.

monoculture
An area in which a single species of plant is growing.

national quota
A country's share of the total allowable catch.

natural fertiliser
A fertiliser made from naturally occurring organic substances, such as farmyard manure.

natural yield
The biomass that can be harvested from a population without reducing the population size; it is equal to the amount by which the biomass of the population would increase if no harvesting took place.

nature conservation
Conservation that focuses on maintaining a wide variety of habitats.

non-selective herbicide
A non-selective herbicide is one that harms many different plants, not just the targeted plant. Also called a broad-spectrum herbicide.

open systems
An open system of aquaculture grows fish in near-natural conditions.

organic farming
A method of farming in which no synthetic fertilisers, pesticides or herbicides are used.

outbreeding
Breeding between unrelated individuals; it helps to maintain genetic diversity.

ozone layer
An area in the high atmosphere in which ozone is present; this ozone absorbs much of the potentially damaging ultraviolet radiation from the sun that would otherwise reach the Earth's surface.

parasitism
Feeding on another organism, where the parasite lives in close association with the organism on which it feeds, and does harm to it.

pelagic fish
Fish that swim in open water.

PEP carboxylase
An enzyme found in C_4 plants, which catalyses the combination of carbon dioxide with PEP.

percentage cover
The percentage of the area within a quadrat that is occupied by a particular species.

persistence
A measure of how long a substance lasts within the environment.

pests
Organisms that damage crops or cause disease to farmed animals.

pesticide
A substance that kills pests, such as insects or parasites.

photosynthetic efficiency
The percentage of sunlight energy that is converted into chemical energy by photosynthesis.

pitfall trap
A hole into which small invertebrates may fall as they walk across the ground.

point quadrat
A quadrat that is so small that it covers only one point; useful for collecting reliable data about percentage cover.

pollutant
A substance which, when introduced into the environment, has a harmful effect on living organisms.

pollution
The addition to the environment of substances that are likely to cause harm to living organisms.

polyculture
A system of aquaculture in which several different species are farmed together, for example fish, shellfish and algae.

predation
Catching and feeding on other animals.

primary productivity
The rate at which plants convert sunlight energy into energy in carbohydrates and other organic compounds.

primary succession
Succession that is occurring on a piece of ground where no living organisms were originally present.

quadrat
A defined area of habitat within which data are collected.

random sampling
Collecting information from a number of randomly situated sites within an area; random sampling is used when the area is reasonably uniform in structure.

recruitment
The addition of new individuals to a population, by birth and immigration.

ribulose bisphosphate carboxylase (rubisco)
The enzyme responsible for the fixation of carbon dioxide during photosynthesis.

sampling techniques
Methods of collecting data from a small, representative part of a study area.

secondary succession
Succession that is occurring on a piece of ground which had been disturbed, but where some vegetation remained.

selective herbicide
A selective herbicide is one that kills only the targeted plant.

sere
One of the stages in a succession.

sessile
Tending to remain in one place for a long time; limpets are sessile animals.

Simpson's Diversity Index
A formula for calculating species diversity.

species conservation
Conservation that focuses on saving one particular species from extinction.

species density
The mean number of individuals of a species in a unit area.

GLOSSARY

species richness
The number of different species in a habitat.

SSSI
A Site of Special Scientific Interest, which has some degree of governmental protection.

succession
The gradual, directional change in a community and its habitat over time.

sweep netting
Catching invertebrates by sweeping a net through vegetation.

synergism
The interaction between two factors in which the total effect of both is greater than the addition of their individual effects.

systematic sampling
Collecting information from areas that are especially chosen within an area; systematic sampling is used when investigating a particular gradation or pattern of distribution that may be present in an area.

systemic herbicide
A herbicide that is absorbed through the roots of a plant, and is then transported throughout the plant in the phloem vessels.

taxis
A response in which an animal moves towards or away from a stimulus.

total allowable catch (TAC)
The maximum quantity of a particular species of fish that is allowed to be caught under the rules of the Common Fisheries Policy.

transect
A type of systematic sampling in which data are recorded along a line through the study area.

water meadows
Grassy areas that flood naturally when water levels rise in autumn and winter.

water trap
A container, often brightly-coloured, of water to which flying insects are attracted; detergent is often added to the water so that insects sink and drown.

weeds
Plants growing where they are not wanted.

xerophytes
Plants that are adapted for survival in dry conditions.